The Complete Guide to Godly Play

Volume 4, Revised and Expanded

Jerome W. Berryman

Cheryl V. Minor, Consulting Editor

Rosemary Beales, Consulting Editor

An imaginative method for nurturing the spiritual lives of children

Church Publishing
NEW YORK

© 2018 by Jerome W. Berryman

Consulting Editors: Cheryl V. Minor and Rosemary Beales

Illustrator: Steve Marchesi, pages 163, 186, 189

Any scripture quotations used in this work are from the *Revised Standard Version of the Bible*. Old Testament Section © 1952; New Testament Section, First Edition, © 1946; Second Edition, © 1971 by the Division of Christian Education of the National Council of Churches of Christ in the USA.

A record of this book is available from the Library of Congress.

ISBN-13: 978-0-89869-086-6 (book)

ISBN-13: 978-0-89869-087-3 (ebook)

Contents

Introduction

Welcome to *The Complete Guide to Godly Play, Volume 4, Revised and Expanded*. In this volume, we gather together the presentations that form a suggested cycle of lessons for the season of Lent leading up to Easter. In addition, this volume includes lessons about those who followed Jesus (the men and women), the Holy Eucharist, Pentecost, the Apostle Paul, and the Sacred Story Synthesis Lesson called "The Holy Trinity." The volume concludes with a lesson entitled, "The Part that Hasn't Been Written Yet." Volume 1 of the series, *How to Lead Godly Play Lessons*, provides an in-depth overview of the process and methods of Godly Play. Another important resource that provides a detailed overview of this approach is *Teaching Godly Play: How to Mentor the Spiritual Development of Children*, by Jerome Berryman. Below you will find quick reminder notes.

What Is Godly Play?

Godly Play is what Jerome Berryman calls his interpretation of Montessori religious education. It is an imaginative approach for working with children, an approach that supports, challenges, nourishes, and guides their spiritual quest. It is more akin to spiritual guidance than to what we generally think of as religious education.

Godly Play assumes that children have some experience of the mystery of the presence of God in their lives but that they lack the language, permission, and understanding to express and enjoy that in our culture.

In Godly Play, we enter into Parables, Silence, Sacred Stories, and Liturgical Action in order to discover the depths of God, ourselves, one another, and the world around us. In Godly Play, we prepare a special environment for children to work in with adult guides. Two adults (a storyteller and a doorperson) guide the session, making time for the children to do the following:

- Enter the space and be greeted.
- Get ready for the presentation (a story or lesson).
- Enter into a presentation based on a Parable, Sacred Story, or Liturgical Action.
- Respond to the presentation through shared wondering.
- Respond to the presentation (or other significant spiritual issues) with their own work, either expressive art or with the other materials on the shelves.

- Prepare and share a feast.
- Say goodbye and leave the space.

To help understand what Godly Play is, we can also take a look at what Godly Play is not. First, Godly Play is not a complete children's program. Christmas pageants, vacation Bible school, children's choirs, children's and youth groups, parent-child retreats, picnics, service opportunities, week-day programs, and other components of a full and vibrant children's ministry are all important and are not in competition with Godly Play. What Godly Play contributes to the glorious mix of activities is the heart of the matter, the art of knowing and knowing how to use the language of the Christian people to make meaning about life and death. Godly Play is different from many other approaches to children's work with Scripture. One popular approach is having fun with Scripture. That's an approach we might find in many church school pageants, vacation Bible schools, or other such suggested children's activities.

Having fun with Scripture is fine, but children also need deeply respectful experiences with Scripture if they are to fully enter into its power. If we leave out the heart of the matter, we risk trivializing the Christian way of life and will miss the profound satisfaction of existential discovery, a kind of "fun" that keeps us truly alive.

How Do You Do Godly Play?

When doing Godly Play, be patient. With time, your own style, informed by the practices of Godly Play, will emerge. Even if you use another curriculum for church school, you can begin to incorporate aspects of Godly Play into your practice—beginning with elements as simple as the greeting and goodbye.

Please pay careful attention to the environment you provide for children. The Godly Play environment is an open environment in the sense that children may make genuine choices regarding both the materials they use and the process by which they work. The Godly Play environment is a boundaried environment in the sense that children are protected and guided to make constructive choices.

As guides, we set nurturing boundaries for the Godly Play environment by managing time, space, and relationships in a clear and firm way. The setting needs such limits to be the kind of safe place in which a creative encounter with God can flourish. Let's explore each of these ways to nurture in greater depth.

How to Manage Time

An Ideal Session

A full Godly Play session takes one to two hours and has four parts. These four parts echo the way most Christians organize their worship together.

Opening: Entering the Space and Building the Circle

The storyteller sits in the circle, waiting for the children to enter. The doorperson helps children and parents separate outside the room and helps the children slow down as they cross the threshold. The storyteller helps each child sit in a specific place in the circle and greets each child warmly by name.

The storyteller, by modeling and direct instruction, helps the children get ready for the day's presentation.

Hearing the Word of God: Presentation and Response

The storyteller first invites a child to move the hand of the church "clock" wall hanging to the next block of color (see Volume 2, Lesson 1, The Circle of the Church Year, on page 27 for a complete description of this). The storyteller then presents the day's lesson. At the presentation's end, the storyteller invites the children to wonder together about the lesson. The storyteller then goes around the circle asking each child to choose work for the day. If necessary, the doorperson helps children get out their work, either storytelling materials or art supplies. As the children work, some might remain with the storyteller who presents another lesson or story to them. This smaller group is made up of those who are not able to choose their own work yet.

Sharing the Feast: Preparing the Feast and Sharing It in Holy Leisure

The doorperson helps three children set out the feast—such as juice, water, fruit or cookies—for the children to share. Children take turns saying prayers, whether silently or aloud, until the storyteller says the last prayer. The children and storyteller share the feast, clean things up, and put the waste in the trash.

Dismissal: Saying Goodbye and Leaving the Space

The children get ready to say goodbye. The doorperson calls each child by name to say goodbye to the storyteller. The storyteller holds out his or her hands, letting the child make the decision to hug, hold hands, or not touch at all. The storyteller says goodbye and reflects on the pleasure of having the child in this community.

When you have a full hour to work with, the opening, presentation of the lesson, and wondering aloud together about the lesson might take about twenty minutes. The children's response to the lesson through art, retelling, and other work might take about twenty-five minutes. Preparing the feast, sharing the feast, and saying goodbye might take another twenty minutes.

If You Only Have the Famous Forty-Five Minute Hour

You may have a limited time for your session—as little as forty-five minutes instead of two hours. With a forty-five-minute session, you have several choices.

Focus on the Feast

Sometimes, children take especially long to get ready. If you need a full fifteen minutes to build the circle, you can move directly to the feast, leaving time for a leisurely goodbye. You will not shortchange the children. The quality of time and relationships that the children experience within the space is the most important lesson presented in a Godly Play session.

Focus on the Word

Most often, you will have time for a single presentation, including time for the children and you to respond to the lesson by wondering together. Finish with the feast and then the goodbye ritual. Because the children have not had time to make a work response, we suggest that every three or four sessions, you omit any presentation and focus on the work instead (see the next section).

Focus on the Work

If you usually pass from the presentation directly to the feast, then every three or four sessions, substitute a work session for a presentation. First, build the circle. Then, without making a presentation, help children choose their work for the day. Allow enough time at the end of the session to share the feast and say goodbye.

Planning Church Year

When you first get started, and thereafter with your youngest children, you will only need the Core Lessons. Most of the Godly Play Core Lessons are found in Volumes 2, 3, and 4. There is another Core Lesson in Volume 7 and a few found in Volume 8. Most of these are on the top shelf in your room, so you can put beautiful picture books and other things such as maps and artifacts on the lower shelves. As the children (and storytellers) become fluent in the Core Lessons (we think that begins to happen after three encounters with a lesson), you can start to add Extension and Enrichment Lessons. These lessons are below the lessons they extend or enrich, thus filling out your shelves.

The scheduling of these lessons depends on your program year. In the Northern Hemisphere, for example, the program year generally follows the school year, which begins in September and ends around the beginning of June. We suggest you begin with the lessons in Volume 2, starting with the Circle of the Church Year, the Bible, and then the Old Testament stories from Creation through the Prophets. In winter, you can present the Advent, Christmas, and Epiphany lessons followed by the Parables (Volume 3). In spring, we suggest the Faces of Christ (Volume 4) or the Greatest Parable (Volume 8), followed by Easter presentations of the resurrection (Volumes 4 and 8), the Eucharist, and people of the early Church. You will also want to include the lesson on baptism (Volume 3), perhaps on a Sunday when the whole community will celebrate baptisms, and you might want to add some of the lessons about the saints (Volume 7) when appropriate.

As you begin to add Extension and Enrichment Lessons for experienced "Godly Players," scheduling gets more complicated, because you never want to leave the Core Lessons behind altogether and there are many lessons. One year you might decide to focus on some of the people in the first five books of the Bible, beginning with the Core Lesson on the Great Family (Volume 2), and then going to the lessons that extend that lesson—Abraham, Sarah, Jacob, and Joseph. The next year you might decide to introduce some of the individual Prophets in Volume 6. Start by telling the Core Lesson on the Prophets (Volume 2) and then tell Elijah, Isaiah, Jeremiah, and Ezekiel (all Extension Lessons) from Volume 6.

In the parts of the world where the school year begins in late January or early February and ends in December, you will start the year quite differently. Judyth Roberts, a Godly Play trainer in Australia, says they often begin with the Faces of Christ (Volume 3) in February, and then after Easter tell the Old Testament stories, and so on. No matter what, the same principles apply: start with the Core Lessons, adding the Extension and Enrichment Lessons after the children and storytellers are fluent in the Core Lessons, which takes about three encounters with a lesson.

Other important things to consider are the following:

- Groups with regularly scheduled short sessions will need to substitute work sessions for presentations every third or fourth Sunday.
- If the storyteller is not yet comfortable with a particular presentation, we recommend substituting a work session for that day's presentation.
- Within a work session, one child might ask a question that draws on an Enrichment Lesson; for example, "Why do we have crosses in church?" That is a teachable moment to bring out the lesson on crosses (Volume 4, Lesson 9).

How to Manage Space

Getting Started

We strongly recommend you attend a Godly Play Foundation training or consult with a Godly Play Foundation Trainer. If you live outside of the United States, please contact the Godly Play Foundation to get in touch with the Godly Play organizations closest to you. You can find a listing of Trainers at www.godlyplayfoundation.org. We also recommend a thorough reading of *Teaching Godly Play: How to Mentor the Spiritual Development of Children* by Jerome Berryman, and *The Complete Guide to Godly Play, Volume 1: How to Lead Godly Play Lessons.*

To start, focus on the relationships and actions that are essential to Godly Play, rather than on the materials needed in a fully equipped Godly Play space. We know that not every congregation can allocate generous funds for Christian education. We believe Godly Play is worth beginning with the simplest of resources. Without any materials at all, two teachers can make a Godly Play space that greets the children, shares a feast, and blesses them goodbye each week.

When Jerome and Thea Berryman began their work with children, Jerome and Thea used shelving made from boards and cinder blocks. They created a new material each week. The first one was the Parable of the Good Shepherd, which they cut from construction paper and placed in a shoebox spray painted gold.

During that first year, Berryman filled the shelves with more homemade lesson materials. When more time and money became available, he upgraded those materials to some cut from foam core. Now his research room is fully equipped with beautiful and lasting Godly Play materials: Parable Boxes, Noah's Ark, a Desert Box filled with sand, and more. All of these riches are wonderful gifts to the children who spend time there, but the start of a successful Godly Play environment is the nurturing of appropriate relationships in a safe place with the best materials you can manage at the time.

Materials

Materials for Presentations

Each lesson details the materials needed in a section titled "Notes on the Material." You can make materials yourself, or you can order beautifully crafted and official materials licensed by the Godly Play Foundation, including less expensive kits for making the materials yourself. Several countries have licensed organizations making materials. A brief list follows. For a complete, up-to-date list, go to www.godlyplayfoundation.org.

United States
Godly Play Resources
P.O. Box 563
Ashland, KS 67831
Phone: (800) 445-4390
Fax: (620) 635-2191
E-mail: info@godlyplayresources.com
www.godlyplayresources.com

England
St. Michael's Workshop
Bowthorpe Hall Road
Norwich NR5 9AA
Phone: 01603 746106
www.stmichaelsworkshop.co.uk

Germany
Diakonisches Werk Innere Mission
Leipzig e.V.
Lindenwerkstätten WfbM II
An den Werkstätten 4
04451 Borsdorf | OT Panitzsch
Phone: 034291. 44 02 50
E-mail: lindenwfb-panitzsch@
    diakonie-leipzig.de
www.godlyplay-materialien.de/

Here is a list a list of all suggested materials for the presentations in Volume 4:

Throughout the year (for all or many of the lessons):

- Circle of the Church Year (wall hanging)
- Cloths in liturgical colors (white, purple, red, green, blue)
- Holy Family and the Risen Christ figures (See *Volume 2*, Lesson 3.)
- Juice or water, fruit, cookies, or crackers
- Matzo (should always be available if you have told *Volume 2*, Lesson 7)

Lesson 1: The Mystery of Easter

- Purple and white bag
- Six puzzle pieces (the pieces form a cross)
- A tray to hold the bag

Lesson 2: The Faces of Easter I

- Seven plaques showing the Faces of Christ (the seventh one is two-sided)
- A strip of felt consisting of six purple segments and one white segment—rolled with the white on the inside
- A stand or tray to hold the plaques

Lesson 3: The Faces of Easter II

- Seven plaques showing the Faces of Christ (the seventh one is two-sided)
- A strip of felt consisting of six purple segments and one white segment—rolled with the white on the inside
- A stand or tray to hold the plaques

Lesson 4: The Faces of Easter III

- Seven plaques showing the Faces of Christ (the seventh one is two-sided)
- A strip of felt consisting of six purple segments and one white segment—rolled with the white on the inside
- A stand or tray to hold the plaques

Lesson 5: The Faces of Easter IV

- Seven plaques showing the Faces of Christ (the seventh one is two-sided)
- A strip of felt consisting of six purple segments and one white segment—rolled with the white on the inside
- A stand or tray to hold the plaques

Lesson 6: The Faces of Easter V

- Seven plaques showing the Faces of Christ (the seventh one is two-sided)
- A strip of felt consisting of six purple segments and one white segment—rolled with the white on the inside
- A stand or tray to hold the plaques

Lesson 7: The Faces of Easter VI

- Seven plaques showing the Faces of Christ (the seventh one is two-sided)
- A strip of felt consisting of six purple segments and one white segment—rolled with the white on the inside
- A stand or tray to hold the plaques

Lesson 8: The Faces of Easter VII

- Seven plaques showing the Faces of Christ (the seventh one is two-sided)
- A strip of felt consisting of six purple segments and one white segment—rolled with the white on the inside
- A stand or tray to hold the plaques

Lesson 9: The Crosses

- Collection of crosses in a container
- Rug or felt underlay
- *Optional*: cards showing and/or explaining the crosses

Lesson 10: The Legend of the Easter Eggs

- Large Wooden Tray
- Small Wooden Tray holding one Ukrainian Easter egg in a translucent box
- The tray also holds a small basket of two-dimensional, egg-shaped samples of colors, designs, and patterns
- One real (or wooden) egg in a small basket covered with a white cloth
- Rug

Lesson 11: Jesus and the Twelve

- Picture of the Last Supper mounted on wood or foam core
- Symbols for the Twelve Apostles mounted on wood or laminated
- Control card

Lesson 12: The Good Shepherd and World Communion

- Figures of the Good Shepherd, sheep, sheepfold, table, priest, and people of the world
- Small container holding a small paten and chalice
- Two circles of green felt mounted on wood

Lesson 13: The Synagogue and the Upper Room

- Model of a synagogue, with a scroll in a basket and a lectern
- Model of the Upper Room with a table
- Figure of Jesus

Lesson 14: The Circle of the Holy Eucharist

- Wooden tray
- Card or wooden plaque picturing Jesus in the Upper Room
- Card or wooden plaque picturing Jesus in the synagogue
- Set of seventeen cards or wooden plaques showing the major parts of the Eucharist
- Green felt circle

Lesson 15: Symbols of the Holy Eucharist

- Wooden liturgical furnishings (tabernacle, credence table, lectern, altar, pulpit, sacristy cupboard)
- Cloth furnishings (seasonal hangings, fair linen, purificators)
- Other furnishings (Bible, candles, candle sticks, candle snuffer, altar book, Gospel Book, cruets for water and wine, ciborium, chalice, paten)
- Box of prompting cards

Lesson 16: The Mystery of Pentecost

- Red Parable-sized box
- Twelve brown strips
- Six plain wooden blocks
- Symbols of the Twelve Apostles mounted on wood or laminated

Lesson 17: Saul Changes

- Wooden tray
- Red road
- Two blocks of wood to represent the cities of Jerusalem and Damascus
- A wooden plaque with an illustration of the event on the road to Damascus
- Tan felt underlay

Lesson 18: Paul's Travels and His Letters

- Wooden tray containing seven cards or wooden plaques illustrating scenes from Paul's life (including the plaque in Lesson 17)
- Thirteen scrolls
- Red strip of cloth or felt

Lesson 19: The Holy Trinity

- Materials from the Creation presentation (*The Complete Guide to Godly Play, Volume 2*, Lesson 4)
- Materials from the Faces of Easter presentations (this volume, Lessons 2–8)
- Materials from Paul's Travels and His Letters presentation (this volume, Lesson 18)
- Three white circles from the Holy Baptism presentation (*The Complete Guide to Godly Play, Volume 3*, Lesson 8)

Lesson 20: The Part That Hasn't Been Written Yet

- Book stand
- Blank book

Materials for Children's Work

Gather art supplies that the children can use to make their responses. These materials are kept on the art shelves. We suggest the following:

- Rugs or mats in a basket or box
- Kneeling tables (low tables children can kneel at when working with materials such as clay)

- Paper of various sizes and kinds
- Large and small trays
- Paint and brushes
- Drawing boards
- Crayons, pencils, and markers
- Clay rolled into small balls in airtight containers

Materials for the Feast
- Napkins (small "cocktail size" napkins in liturgical colors—green, purple, red, white, and blue)
  - Many Godly Play programs have adopted a "green feast" using re-usable cloth napkins and cups.
- Serving basket
- Cups
- Tray
- Pitcher

Materials for Cleanup
Gather cleaning materials that the children can use to clean up after their work and care for their environment. We suggest the following:

- Paper towels
- Feather duster
- Brush and dustpan
- Cleaning cloths
- Spray bottles with water
- Trash can with liner

How to Arrange Materials
The materials are arranged to communicate visually and silently the language system of the Christian faith: our Sacred Stories, Parables, and our Liturgical Action. Main Core Presentations are generally kept on the top shelves.

Enrichment and Extension Presentations are generally kept on the second and third shelves under the story they enrich or extend. These lower shelves also hold supplemental materials, such as books, maps, or other resources. Separate shelves hold supplies for art, cleanup, and the feast. A shelf for children's work in progress is also very important.

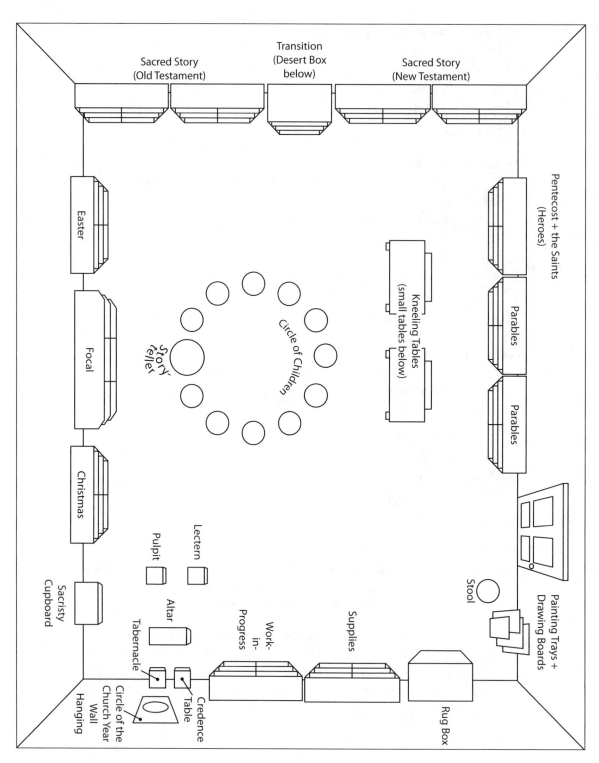

A Map of a Godly Play Room

How to Manage Relationships

The Two Adult Guides: Doorperson and Storyteller

Each adult guide fosters respect for the children and the Godly Play space. For example, parents are left at the threshold of the Godly Play space, and teachers remain at the children's eye level. Both practices keep the room child-centered, instead of adult-centered.

Similarly when the storyteller presents a lesson, he or she keeps his or her eyes focused on the materials of the lesson—not the children. Instead of being encouraged to respond to an adult, the children are invited, by the storyteller's eyes, to enter the story. In a typical Godly Play session, only two adults will be present: the doorperson and the storyteller. These are their respective tasks during a typical session:

Doorperson	Storyteller
	Check the material to be presented that day.
Check the shelves, especially the supply shelves and art shelves. Prepare the feast so that you will not have to work on that during the session.	
	Get seated on the floor in the circle, and prepare to greet the children.
Get out the roll book, review notes, and get ready to greet the children and parents. Slow down the children coming into the room. Help them to get ready. Take the roll, or have the older children check themselves in. You may need to put aside toys, books, and other distracting objects.	
	Guide the children to places in the circle where they will best be able to attend to the lesson. Visit quietly until it is time to begin and all are ready.
Close the door when it is time. Be ready to work with latecomers and children who come to you from the circle.	
	Present the lesson. Model how to "enter" the material.

Avoid casual eye contact with the storyteller to help prevent the adults in the room from turning the children into objects, talking down to them, or manipulating them.

Draw the children into the lesson by your introduction. Bring your gaze down to focus on the material when you begin the actual lesson. Look up when the wondering begins.

After the lesson and wondering, put the lesson away. Model how to care for the material, and remind them where it should be placed on the shelves. Then go around the circle, dismissing each child to begin his or her work, one at a time. Each child chooses what to do. Go quickly around the circle the first time, returning to the children who did not decide. Go around the circle for decisions until only a few are left—who may be new or for some other reason cannot make a choice. Present a lesson to these children.

When the children choose their work, listen so that you can help them get out their work. They may need help setting up artwork and getting materials from the shelves for work on a lesson, either alone or in a group.

Remain seated in the circle unless children need help with the lessons they have gotten out. You may need to help with art materials. Keep yourself at the children's eye level when you help.

Stay in your chair unless children need your help. Do not intrude on the community of children. Stay at the eye level of the children whenever possible, as if there is a glass ceiling in the room at the level of the taller children.

When it is time for the feast, go to the light switch and turn it off. Ask the children to put their work away and come back to the circle for the feast. Turn the light back on. Go to the circle to anchor it as the children finish their work and return.

Help the children put their work away, and invite some of the children who finish early to help with the feast.

Ask for prayers, but do not pressure. After the feast, show the children how to put their things away in the trash or on a tray for washing if you use reusable napkins and cups.

Sit quietly in your chair, but be sure that the trash can has a liner in it. Greet the parents and begin to call the names of the children who are ready and whose parents are there. Remember to give back anything that may have been taken at the beginning of class.

As the children's names are called, they come to you. Hold out your hands. Children can take your hands, give a hug or keep their distance, as they like. Tell them quietly and privately how glad you were to see them and what good work they did today. Invite them to come back when they can. Take time to enjoy saying goodbye, with all the warmth of a blessing for each child.

If a child starts for the door without saying goodbye to the storyteller, remind him or her to return to the storyteller to say goodbye.

When all are gone, check the material shelves and clean.

When the children are gone, check and clean the art and supply shelves.

Sit quietly and contemplate the class as a whole.

Evaluate, make notes, and discuss the session with the storyteller.

Sit quietly and contemplate the class as a whole.

Evaluate, make notes, and discuss the session with the doorperson.

Learning the Stories by Heart

Godly Play lessons are meant to be learned "by heart," not memorized. When a story sinks into your heart, it also comes from your heart in the telling. Children know the difference. When we present the story from the heart it removes the distraction of having to look in two different places—the text and the materials—as you present the story. (Focusing your visual attention on the materials helps you remember the language. It gives the children only one place to look—at the story materials. This focuses their attention as well as yours.)

We suggest that storytellers begin by reading the story in the Bible, and then study the script. It is also helpful to read through all the lessons to look for repeated phrases. These you may want to memorize for consistency sake. For help in learning how to use the materials, we recommend the Godly Play Foundation's official YouTube channel, which you can find by going to www. godlyplayfoundation.org or www.youtube.com/user/GodlyPlayFndn/videos. There you will be able to see Godly Play Trainers present the lessons.

How Others Can Help

Other adults who want to support the work of a Godly Play program can contribute by:

- Taking turns providing simple and healthy food for the children to share during their feasts
- Keeping the art and supply shelves replenished with fresh materials
- Using their creative skills to make materials for Godly Play presentations

How to Respond Effectively to Disruptions in the Circle

You always want to model the behavior you expect in the circle: focused on the lesson and respectful of everyone in the circle. If a disruption occurs, you deal with that disruption in such a way that you still show continual respect for everyone in the circle—including the child who is having trouble that day. You also still maintain as much focus on the lesson as you can, returning to complete focus on the lesson as quickly as possible.

Therefore, as you consider responses, remember to keep a neutral tone in your voice. Remember, too, that our goal is to help the child move himself or herself toward more appropriate behavior. At the first level of interruption, you might simply raise your eyes from the material. You look up, but not directly at the child, while saying, "We need to get ready again. Watch. This is how we get ready." Model the way to get ready, and begin again the presentation where you left off.

If the interruption continues or increases, address the child directly. Tell them the following: "No, that's not fair. Look at all these children who are listening. They are ready. You need to be ready, too. Let's try again. Good. That's the way." If the interruption continues or increases, ask the child to sit by the doorperson. Don't think of this as a punishment or as an exclusion from the story: some children want to sit by the doorperson for their own reasons. Continue to keep a neutral tone of voice as you say, "I think you need to sit, by Ann (use the doorperson's name). You can see and hear from there. The lesson is still for you."

The goal is for the child to take himself or herself to the door. If the child is having trouble, or says, "No" you can say, "May I help you?" Only if necessary, help him or her go to the doorperson.

How to Support the Children's Work
Show respect for the children's work in two key ways: Through the structure of the space and the language you use—and do not use—in talking about their work. Let's explore each of these.

A Godly Play Room's Structure
A Godly Play Room is structured to support children's work in four ways:

- First, it makes materials inviting and available by keeping the room open, clean, and well organized. A useful phrase for a Godly Play Room is, "This material is for you. You can touch this and work with this when you want to. If you haven't had the lesson, ask one of the other children or the storyteller to show it to you." Children walking into a Godly Play Room take delight at all the fascinating materials calling out to them. These materials say, "This room is for you."
- Second, it encourages responsible stewardship of the shared materials by helping children learn to take care of the room themselves. When something spills, we could quickly wipe it up ourselves, of course. Instead, by helping children learn to take care of their own spills, we communicate to them the respect we have for their own problem-solving capabilities. At the end of work time, each child learns to put away materials carefully. In fact, some children may want to choose cleaning work—dusting or watering plants—for their entire response time.

- Third, it provides a respectful place for children's work by reserving space in the room for ongoing or finished projects. When a child is still working on a project at the end of work time, reassure him or her by saying, "This project will be here for you next time you come. You can take as many weeks as you need to finish it. We never lose work in a Godly Play Room." Sometimes, children want to give a finished piece of work to the room. Sometimes, children want to take either finished or unfinished work home. These choices are theirs to make and ours to respect.

- Fourth, it sets a leisurely pace that allows children to engage deeply in their chosen responses. This is why it's better to do no more than build the circle, share a feast, and lovingly say goodbye when we are pressed for time rather than rush through a story and time of art response. When we tell a story, we want to allow enough time for leisurely wondering together. When we provide work time, we want to allow enough time for children to become deeply engaged in their work. In their wondering or their work, children may be dealing with deep issues—issues that matter as much as life and death. Provide them a nourishing space filled with safe time for this deep work.

Using Language

You can also support children with the language you use:

- Choose "open" responses. We choose "open" responses when we simply describe what we see rather than evaluate the children or their work. Open responses invite children's interaction but respect children's choices to simply keep working in silence, too. Examples include the following:

1. Hm. Lots of red.

2. This is big work. The paint goes all the way from here to there.

3. This clay looks so smooth and thin now.

- Avoid evaluation. Evaluative responses shift the child's focus from his or her work to your praise. In a Godly Play Room, we want to allow children the freedom to work on what matters most to them, not for the reward of our praise. Examples of evaluative responses include the following:

1. You're a wonderful painter.

2. This is a great picture.

3. I'm so pleased with what you did.

- Choose empowering responses, which emphasize each child's ability to make choices, solve problems, and articulate needs. In a Godly Play Room, a frequently heard phrase is, "That's the way. You can do this." We encourage children to choose their own work, get the materials out carefully, and clean up their work areas when they are done. When a child spills something, respond with, "That's no problem. Do you know where the cleanup supplies are kept?" If a child needs help, show where the supplies are kept or how to wring out a sponge. When helping, the aim is to restore ownership of the problem or situation to the child as soon as possible.

- Stay alert to children's needs during work and cleanup time. The doorperson's role is especially important as children get out and put away their work. By staying alert to the children's choices in the circle, the doorperson can know when to help a new child learn the routine for using clay, when a child might need help moving the Desert Box, or when a child might need support in putting material away or cleaning up after painting.

More Information on Godly Play

The Complete Guide to Godly Play, Volumes 1–8 by Jerome W. Berryman are available from Church Publishing Incorporated in New York. *Teaching Godly Play: How to Mentor the Spiritual Development of Children* by Jerome W. Berryman, also available from Church Publishing, is the essential handbook for using Godly Play in church school or a wide variety of alternative settings. In the Appendix of this volume, you will find a complete listing of the foundational literature for Godly Play.

Church Publishing also sells the Godly Play lessons digitally, either as single lessons or by compilation, such as The Faces of Easter. Most lessons also have a corresponding "Parent-Page," which you can purchase digitally from Church Publishing (grouped according to *The Complete Guide to Godly Play* volume) and then make as many copies as you need each time the lesson is presented in your setting. These can also be e-mailed to families in your congregation, but they should not be put on your church's website. All of these can be found at www.churchpublishing.org/godlyplaydigital.

The Godly Play Foundation is the nonprofit organization that sponsors ongoing research, training, and development. The Godly Play Foundation maintains a schedule of training and events related to Godly Play, as well as a list of trainers available throughout the United States and other countries for help in establishing Godly Play programs. Godly Play Resources crafts beautiful and lasting materials, officially licensed for use in a Godly Play Room. The Godly Play Foundation licenses organizations across the globe to produce approved lesson materials. For a complete listing, go to the website of the Godly Play Foundation.

Contact information:
Godly Play Foundation
www.godlyplayfoundation.org

Godly Play Resources
www.GodlyPlayResources.com

Lesson 1

The Mystery of Easter

Lent, the Mystery of Easter, and the Easter Season

How to Use This Lesson

- Enrichment Presentation—This kind of lesson goes over the same material in a Core Lesson but from a different angle or in a more detailed way.
- Liturgical Action Lesson—Lessons about sacraments or traditions of the church, which primarily use ritual and symbol to make meaning.
- This Enrichment Lesson in Volume 4 of *The Complete Guide to Godly Play* adds to the Core Lesson for Lent called "The Faces of Easter." The cross in this lesson will remind the children of the cross that Jesus saw when he first looked up into the faces of Mary and Joseph, and of his journey to the cross—a journey we all take with him every year during the season of Lent.
- As the first lesson in Volume 4 of *The Complete Guide to Godly Play*, it is usually presented at the beginning of Lent.
- It is part of a comprehensive approach to Christian formation that consists of eight volumes. Together the lessons form a spiral curriculum that enables children to move into adolescence with an inner working knowledge of the classical Christian language system to sustain them all their lives.

The Material

- Location: Lent/Easter Shelf Unit
- Pieces: Reversible purple and white bag, six puzzle pieces that form a cross (purple on one side, white on the other), a wooden tray
- Underlay: Use a rug or plain felt underlay

Background

Lent is the season when we prepare for Easter. These six weeks are a solemn time, overflowing with meaning, when we view life from the perspective of our existential limits and the sacrifice of Christ. This lesson gives an introduction to the relationship of Lent to the Mystery of Easter as well as how Easter overflows into the *season* of Easter.

There are several possible uses for this lesson:

- Present it on the Sunday before Lent.
- Present it at a gathering of the congregation on Shrove Tuesday (the night before Lent begins). If you do this you might consider enlarging the material so it's easier to see in a large group setting.

- Present it as part of a liturgy designed for children on Ash Wednesday. This liturgy might include this presentation, a demonstration of how the ashes are made each year (by burning some of the previous year's palms from Palm Sunday), a song, a prayer, and then the imposition of ashes.
- Present it on the First Sunday of Lent, after focusing on the change of seasons.
  - Use The Holy Family presentation (*Volume 2*, Lesson 3) to change the focal shelf color from green to purple.
  - Then tell "The Mystery of Easter."
  - The next week (the second Sunday in Lent) you can either present the first two of "The Faces of Easter" (*Volume 4*, Lessons 2 and 3), or begin the four-part series called "The Greatest Parable" (*Volume 8*, Lessons 1–4).

Notes on the Material

Find the materials for this presentation on the second shelf of the Lent/Easter Shelf Unit, directly under the lesson called "The Faces of Easter" (*Volume 4*, Lessons 2–8).

A bag, which is purple on the outside and white on the inside, holds six puzzle pieces, which, when assembled, make the shape of the cross. One side of the cross is purple; the other side of the cross is white. It is much more than a puzzle with pieces that fit together, as you will see at the end of The Mystery of Easter lesson.

Special Notes

Remember that this story is called "The Mystery of *Easter*," not "The Mystery of Lent." The fullest meaning of Lent is that it gives us time to prepare for the great Mystery of Easter, the principal feast of the Christian Church. Similarly, we recommend that you not call the material a "cross puzzle" but always refer to it as "the material for the Mystery of Easter."

At the end of this lesson the storyteller will put the pieces of the cross inside the bag, leaving it with the white on the outside. It will stay on the shelf like that through the end of that session. However, after the children leave the storyteller should turn the bag back to its purple side so that when the children return the next week they will find a purple bag.

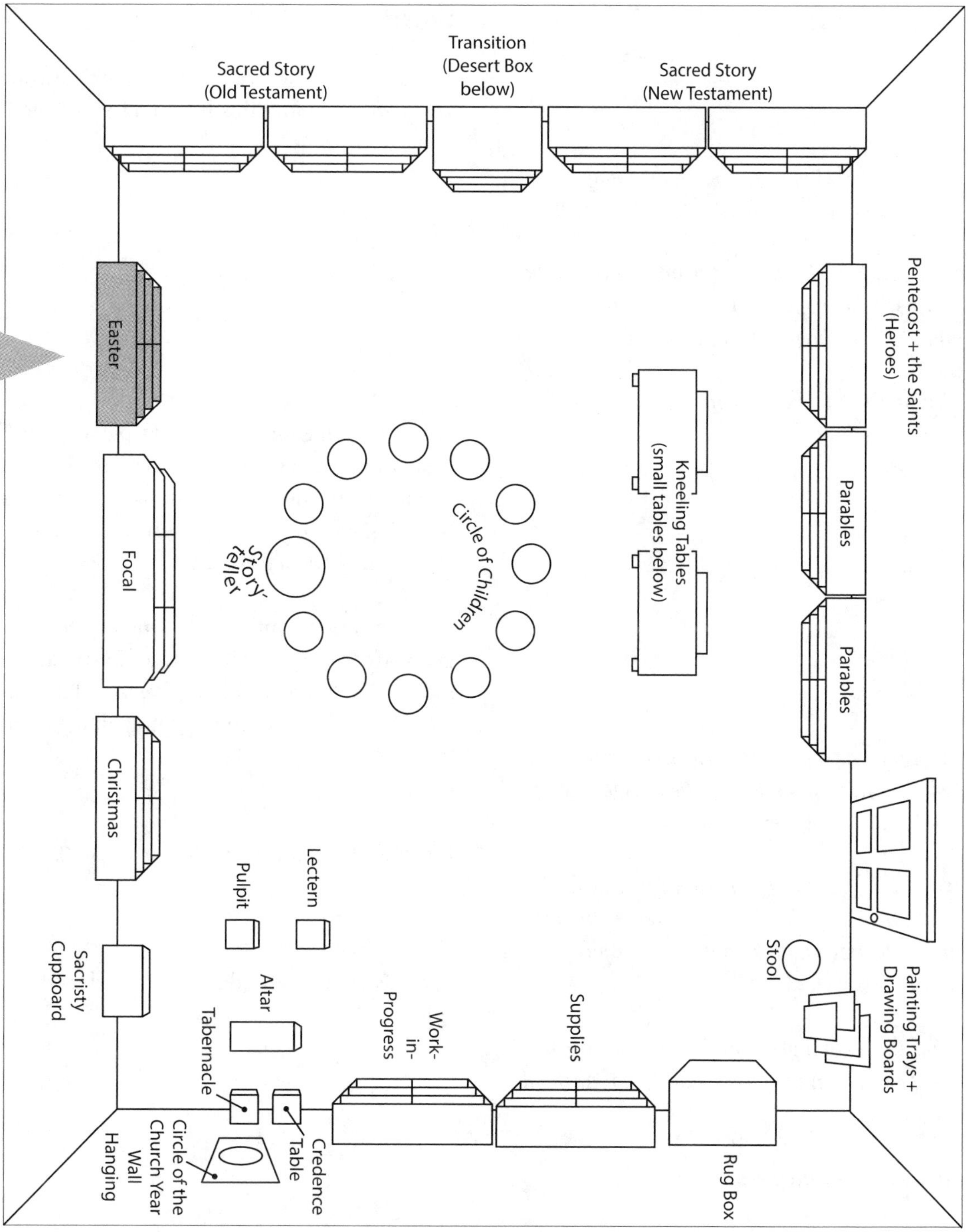
Transition
(Desert Box
below)
Sacred Story
(Old Testament)
Sacred Story
(New Testament)
Easter
Focal
Christmas
Sacristy
Cupboard
Pentecost + the Saints
(Heroes)
Parables
Parables
Kneeling Tables
(small tables below)
Circle of Children
Story-
teller
Lectern
Pulpit
Altar
Tabernacle
Credence
Table
Circle of the
Church Year
Wall
Hanging
Work-
in-
Progress
Supplies
Rug Box
Stool
Painting Trays +
Drawing Boards

Where to Find Materials

Movements

Go to the basket of work rugs in the room and carry one to the circle. Model how to unroll the rug.

Go to the Lent/Easter Shelf Unit and bring the tray with the bag on it. Put the tray at your side and place the bag in the middle of the rug.

Pick up the bag and explore it from the outside.

Place the bag back on the rug and reach inside. Pull out the first piece with the purple side up, taking care not to reveal the white side.

Place it beside the bag. Turn it this way and that. Encourage the children's guesses, then reach inside the bag and take out a second piece.

Place the second piece on the rug, apart from the first piece. Turn the pieces, but do not fit them together.

Take out the third piece.

Put the third piece beside the other two, but do not fit the pieces together. Move the pieces around and try combinations that do not work.

Words

Watch carefully where I go so you will always know where to find this lesson. First we need a rug.

Watch again.

This is the time for the color purple. It is the time for preparing. Purple is the color of kings. We are preparing for the coming of a king and his going and his coming again. We are preparing for the Mystery of Easter.

This is a serious time. It takes many weeks to get ready to enter the Mystery of Easter. Let's look inside to see how many weeks it takes and what Lent makes when you put it all together.

I wonder what this could be?

Look. Here is a second piece. I wonder what this could be?

Look. Here's a third piece.

They are all so different.

Movements	Words
Take out the fourth piece. Put the fourth piece beside the other three, but do not fit the pieces together.	Here is a fourth piece. One, two, three, four weeks in Lent? That's the same as the time for getting ready for Christmas. Perhaps that is all we need for Easter, too.
Take out the fifth piece.	Oh, no! Here's another one. Lent is longer than Advent. I wonder if the Mystery of Easter is an even greater mystery than the Mystery of Christmas. It takes longer to get ready. That must be all there is.
Touch the almost empty bag and "find" yet another piece.	No. It is not empty. There must be another week inside.
Take out the sixth piece.	There is another one! The time of Lent is six weeks. Easter is a huge mystery. Let's see if there is another one.

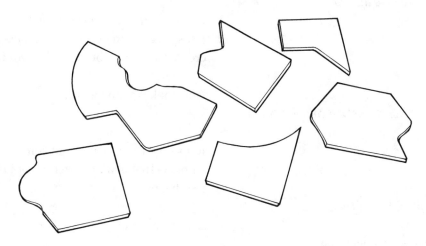

The Pieces of the Cross

Movements	Words
Look in the bag. It is now empty.	Now it is empty. Look. The time of Lent is six weeks.
Place the bag on the floor and sit back to wonder about it.	Lent helps us to get ready. It is a time to know more about the One who is Easter. It is also a time to learn more about who we really are.
Touch one or more of the pieces as you talk about them.	The pieces are very purple.
	The One who is coming is very important, like a king. But purple can feel kind of sad, too. Perhaps what is going to happen is sad.
	I wonder what these make when you put them all together?
Begin to move the pieces around, but do not yet fit them together. Experiment.	
Propose alternative constructions.	
Play. Finally, assemble the cross.	
	Oh, I see. It makes a cross. But it's a sad cross. Jesus grew up to be a man and died on the cross. That is sad, but it is also wonderful.
	Now look what happens.
Turn the pieces over to make a completely white cross.	
	Jesus died on the cross, but somehow he is still with us. That is why Easter is not just sad. It is also happy.
Show the purple side of a few pieces.	Lent is sad . . .
Turn the pieces back to white again.	. . . Easter is pure celebration.

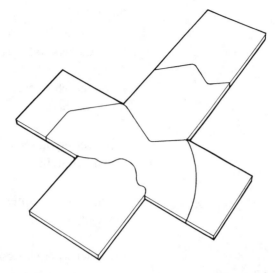

The Assembled Cross (Storyteller's Perspective)

Movements

Reach inside the purple bag and take hold of the inside. Turn the bag inside out.

Count the white pieces.

Sit back and contemplate the Mystery of Easter for a few moments, and then begin the wondering questions.

Words

Easter turns everything inside out and upside down. The color of getting ready becomes the color of pure celebration. The sad seriousness and happiness join together to make joy.

Look! You can't keep Easter in just one Sunday!

It goes on for one, two, three, four, five, six weeks! All the way to Pentecost.

Now I wonder if you have ever seen these colors in the church?

I wonder what happens when you see these colors?

I wonder what part of Lent you like best?

I wonder what part of Lent is the most important?

Movements

When the wondering is finished, put the pieces of the cross inside the bag, leaving it with the white on the outside. Return the material to the shelf and help the children begin to get out their work.

Remember to turn the bag back to the purple side after the children leave so that they will find it that way the next week.

Words

I wonder who takes care of the colors?

I wonder where these colors are when you don't see them?

I wonder if you see the white at some other time in church?

I wonder how sadness and happiness can make joy?

I wonder where joy comes from?

I wonder how you know when joy is here?

I wonder what your work will be today? You might make something about this story, or another story that you know. Maybe you want to work on something else. There are so many things you can choose from. Only you know what is right for you.

Lesson 2

The Faces of Easter I

Jesus' Birth and Growth
(Matthew 1:18–25; Luke 2: 1–7)

How to Use This Lesson

- Core Presentation
- Liturgical Action Lesson: Lessons about sacraments or traditions of the church, which primarily use ritual and symbol to make meaning.
- As the second lesson in Volume 4 of *The Complete Guide to Godly Play*, it is usually presented at the beginning of Lent. It is part of a series of lessons meant to be told over the course of the entire season of Lent.
- It is part of a comprehensive approach to Christian formation that consists of eight volumes. Together the lessons form a spiral curriculum that enables children to move into adolescence with an inner working knowledge of the classical Christian language system to sustain them all their lives.

The Material

- Location: Lent/Easter Shelf Unit
- Pieces: Seven plaques illustrated with Faces of Christ, stand or tray
- Underlay: A strip of felt consisting of seven purple segments and one white segment. The underlay is rolled with the white on the inside.

Background

Lent is the season when we prepare for Easter. This lesson (and the whole series of lessons called "The Faces of Easter") helps children prepare for the Mystery of Easter. We move toward the Mystery by hearing the stories of Christ's journey toward the cross and resurrection. This week's presentation focuses on the face of Christ as a newborn child. If you used the presentations of the Holy Family and the Mystery of Easter on the first week of Lent, then you might want to tell two of the Faces presentations today.

Notes on the Material

Find the materials for this presentation on the left of the top shelf of the Lent/Easter Shelf Unit.

The material consists of a set of seven Faces of Christ, mounted on wood plaques. The underlay is a purple and white "scroll" that unrolls to show six purple rectangles and one white rectangle. Roll up the scroll so that the white rectangle is hidden inside.

A special carrier stand for the Faces plaques stands them up, making them visible to a child scanning the room full of materials. This stand for the plaques also holds the rolled-up scroll. If you do not use this stand, put the rolled-up scroll and plaques on a tray.

Special Notes

At the end of each presentation of the Faces stories, you invite children to choose materials from the room that will help tell more of the story. For example, when you tell today's story of "Jesus' Birth and Growth," one child might bring crèche figures to place by the plaque. Another child might bring the Desert Box. Be open to the surprising connections children make as they explore the meaning embodied in the materials. This activity is especially important because it provides movement and action to these stories and integrates the whole room with Jesus' birth, life, death, and resurrection.

Be sure you unroll the scroll so that its roll is closest to you, not to the children. This keeps the roll from blocking some of the children's view of the Faces. (See the illustration on page 37). As the scroll unrolls, the rolled up portion stays near the storyteller. It is as if the story is growing out of the rolled-up scroll like a seed, the white part rolled up inside. It also is growing out of the storyteller's life and experiences toward the children. The illustrations in these sessions make this clear. Each time you present any of the Faces of Easter, unroll the first section of the scroll, place the first plaque, unroll the second section of the scroll, place the second plaque, etc.

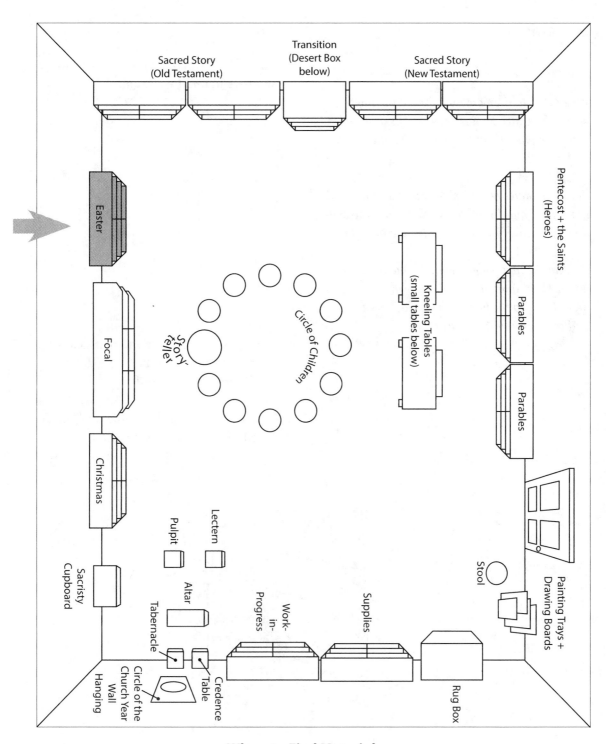

Sacred Story (Old Testament)

Transition (Desert Box below)

Sacred Story (New Testament)

Pentecost + the Saints (Heroes)

Parables

Parables

Easter

Focal

Christmas

Sacristy Cupboard

Story-teller

Circle of Children

Kneeling Tables (small tables below)

Pulpit

Lectern

Altar

Tabernacle

Work-in-Progress

Supplies

Stool

Painting Trays + Drawing Boards

Circle of the Church Year Wall Hanging

Credence Table

Rug Box

Where to Find Materials

Movements

When the children are ready, go to the shelf where the Lent and Easter materials are kept. Bring the plaques and rolled-up underlay "scroll" to the circle.

Put the plaques at your side and place the scroll in front of you. Unroll the scroll toward the children to uncover the rectangle for the first plaque.

Pick up the first plaque, with the picture of the infant Jesus, and hold the face toward the children. Point to the figures as you identify them and trace around their faces.

Words

Watch carefully where I go so you will always know where to find this lesson.

In the beginning, the baby was born. God chose Mary to be the mother of God. Listen carefully! Listen to the words.

God chose Mary to be the mother of God, and the Word was born a wordless child.

Holding the First Plaque (Children's Perspective)

Movements

In Mary's face, trace the cross with your index finger along the line of the nose to the mouth and then the line from eye to eye. Repeat for Joseph's face.

Trace a circle around the whole family.

When you have enjoyed for a moment the idea of the baby growing, put the plaque down on the scroll, facing the children.

Words

When the baby looked up into the face of the Mother Mary, he already saw the cross.

When he looked into the face of the Father Joseph, the cross was there, too.

The Mother Mary and the Father Joseph held the baby close. They kept the baby warm. They gave the baby everything he needed, and the baby began to grow.

Now I wonder if there is anything in this room that you can bring and put beside this picture to help us tell more about this part of the story. Look around and see. I will go around the circle and ask each one of you if you would like to go and get something to put beside the picture of the baby to show more of the story.

The First Plaque on the Underlay (Storyteller's Perspective)

Movements

Begin to go around the circle, asking each child if he or she would like to bring something to put by the plaque.

Some children may not be able to think of anything, so move on if it looks as if they are stuck. You can come back to them later. If they are still stuck, that is okay.

Many children learn by watching as well as by doing.

Sometimes children get up, wander for a moment and bring something at random, without knowing why. That's okay. Be amazed (which is easy) and wonder why with them, together coming up with something relevant. Everything in the room is connected in some way.

Words

I don't know what you are going to get. You are the only one in the world who knows that.

If you don't feel like getting something that's okay. Just enjoy what we make together.

The First Plaque with Items Chosen by the Children (Storyteller's Perspective)

Movements

Enjoy the items that the children bring to help tell the story. When you have had time to enjoy the entire layout, invite children, one at a time, to return their materials to their places on the shelves. Then take the plaques and scroll back to the Lent/Easter Shelf Unit.

Return to your spot in the circle and begin to help the children get out their work.

Words

I wonder what your work will be today? You might make something about this story, or another story that you know. Maybe you want to work on something else.

There are so many things you can choose from. Only you know what is right for you.

Lesson 3

The Faces of Easter II

Jesus is Lost and Found
(Luke 2:41–52)

How to Use This Lesson

- Core Presentation
- Liturgical Action Lesson: Lessons about sacraments or traditions of the church, which primarily use ritual and symbol to make meaning.
- As the third lesson in Volume 4 of *The Complete Guide to Godly Play*, it is usually presented during the season of Lent. It is part of a series of lessons meant to be told over the course of the entire season of Lent.
- It is part of a comprehensive approach to Christian formation that consists of eight volumes. Together the lessons form a spiral curriculum that enables children to move into adolescence with an inner working knowledge of the classical Christian language system to sustain them all their lives.

The Material

- Location: Lent/Easter Shelf Unit
- Pieces: Seven plaques illustrated with faces of Christ, stand or tray
- Underlay: A strip of felt consisting of seven purple segments and one white segment. The underlay is rolled with the white on the inside.

Background

Lent is the season when we prepare for Easter. This lesson continues to help children prepare for the Mystery of Easter. We move toward the Mystery by hearing the stories of Christ's journey toward the cross and resurrection. This week's presentation focuses on the face of Christ as the One who was lost and found.

Begin this week's presentation by presenting a summary of the first plaque, the Face of "Jesus' Birth and Growth" (*Volume 4*, Lesson 2). Then add the second plaque and tell the story found in this second lesson about the Faces of Easter (*Jesus is Lost and Found*).

Since there are seven Faces presentations and only six Sundays in Lent, you may want to combine presentations, telling two or even three stories on a Sunday. Arrange the presentations to fit your church's religious education schedule or other situations.

Notes on the Material

Find the materials for this presentation on the left of the top shelf of the Lent/Easter Shelf Unit.

The material consists of a set of seven Faces of Christ, mounted on wood plaques. The underlay is a purple and white "scroll" that unrolls to show six purple rectangles and one white rectangle. Roll up the scroll so that the white rectangle is hidden inside.

A special carrier stand for the Faces plaques stands them up, making them visible to a child scanning the room full of materials. This stand for the plaques also holds the rolled-up scroll. If you do not use this stand, put the rolled-up scroll and plaques on a tray.

Special Notes

At the end of each presentation of the Faces stories, you invite children to choose materials from the room that will help tell more of the story. This activity helps children perceive connections between the stories. For example, when you tell today's story "*Jesus is Lost and Found*," one child might bring Solomon's Temple to place by the plaque.

Be sure you unroll the scroll so that its roll is closest to you, not to the children. This keeps the roll from blocking some of the children's view of the Faces. The scroll unrolls toward the storyteller; each new plaque will be placed on the scroll closest to the storyteller. This means that you need to slide the scroll away from you to allow room to unroll the next section of the scroll. (See the illustration on page 45.) A child seated across from you can help pull the scroll away from you, with two hands.

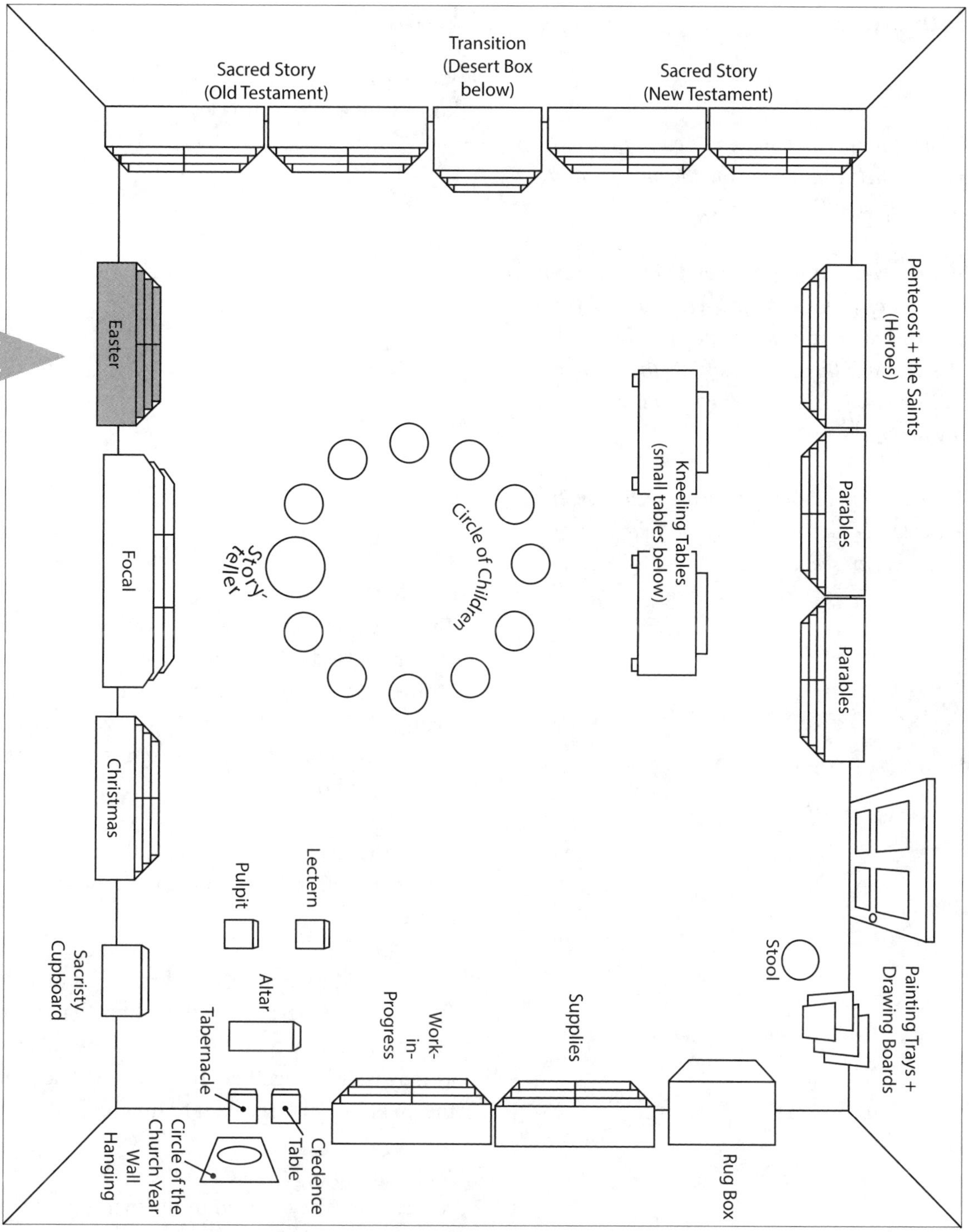
Sacred Story
(Old Testament)
Transition
(Desert Box
below)
Sacred Story
(New Testament)
Pentecost + the Saints
(Heroes)
Parables
Parables
Kneeling Tables
(small tables below)
Circle of Children
Story-
teller
Easter
Focal
Christmas
Lectern
Pulpit
Sacristy
Cupboard
Altar
Tabernacle
Credence
Table
Circle of the
Church Year
Wall
Hanging
Work-
in-
Progress
Supplies
Rug Box
Stool
Painting Trays +
Drawing Boards

Where to Find Materials

Movements

When the children are ready, go to the Lent/ Easter Shelf Unit and bring the plaques and rolled-up scroll to the circle.

Put the cards at your side and place the scroll in front of you. Unroll the scroll toward you to uncover the rectangle for the first plaque. Tell in summary the story "Jesus' Birth and Growth" (Volume 4, Lesson 2). When you are finished, lay down the first plaque.

Unroll the scroll to uncover the second section. Pick up the second plaque and hold it so that the children can see it as you continue the story.

Words

Watch carefully where I go so you will always know where to find this lesson.

The baby grew and became a boy. When he was about twelve years old, he went with the Mother Mary and the Father Joseph and with many other people from their village of Nazareth to the great city of Jerusalem to keep one of the high holy days.

When the celebration was over, the people from Nazareth started on the road toward home.

Suddenly, Mary and Joseph discovered that Jesus was not there! They thought he had been playing with other children from their village as they walked together. They hurried back into the great city of Jerusalem to find him.

Mary and Joseph looked in the dark and narrow streets. They looked in the marketplace where they had bought their food. They looked where they had spent the night. They looked everywhere . . . for three days and three nights!

Movements

Words

Finally, they even looked in the Temple—and there he was, talking to the priests of the Temple. When he spoke, they listened, because he knew so much. When they spoke, he listened, because he wanted to learn more.

Mary and Joseph then asked Jesus the question all parents ask their children, the question you can never answer: "Why did you do this?" And Jesus said something very strange. He said, "Didn't you know I would be in my Father's house?"

Mary and Joseph did not understand. Their house was in Nazareth, where Joseph's carpenter shop was. They did not understand, but they did not forget.

Put the second plaque down on the second rectangle of the scroll, facing the children.

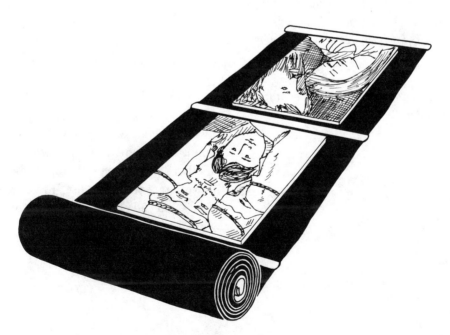

The First and Second Plaques on the Underlay (Storyteller's Perspective)

Movements

Words

Now I wonder what there is in our room that can help us tell more about this story. Look around and see if you see something. I will go around the circle and invite you to go and get something to put by the picture of the boy who was lost and found or the picture of the Christ Child to help us tell more.

Begin to go around the circle, asking each child if he or she would like to bring something to put by the plaque illustrating "Jesus Is Lost and Found" or the previous picture. Some children may not be able to think of anything, so move on if it looks as if they are stuck. You can come back to them later. If they are still stuck, that is okay. Many children learn by watching as well as by doing.

Enjoy the items that the children bring to help tell more of the story. When you have had time to enjoy the entire layout, invite children, one at a time, to return their materials. Then take the plaques and underlay back to the Lent/Easter Shelf Unit.

Return to your spot in the circle and begin to help the children begin to get out their work.

I wonder what your work will be today? You might make something about this story, or another story that you know. Maybe you want to work on something else. There are so many things you can choose from. Only you know what is right for you.

The Faces of Easter III

*Jesus' Baptism and Blessing by God
(Matthew 3:1–17; Mark 1:1–11;
Luke 3: 21–22; John 1:29–34)*

How to Use This Lesson

- Core Presentation
- Liturgical Action Lesson: Lessons about sacraments or traditions of the church, which primarily use ritual and symbol to make meaning.
- As the fourth lesson in Volume 4 of *The Complete Guide to Godly Play*, it is usually presented during the season of Lent. It is part of a series of lessons meant to be told over the course of the entire season of Lent.
- It is part of a comprehensive approach to Christian formation that consists of eight volumes. Together the lessons form a spiral curriculum that enables children to move into adolescence with an inner working knowledge of the classical Christian language system to sustain them all their lives.

The Material

- Location: Lent/Easter Shelf Unit
- Pieces: Seven plaques illustrated with Faces of Christ, stand or tray
- Underlay: A strip of felt consisting of seven purple segments and one white segment. The underlay is rolled with the white on the inside.

Background

Lent is the season when we prepare for Easter. This lesson continues to help children prepare for the Mystery of Easter. We move toward the Mystery by hearing the stories of Christ's journey toward the cross and resurrection. This week's presentation focuses on the Face of Christ as the One who was baptized and blessed.

Begin this week's presentation by presenting a summary of the first two plaques, the Face of "Jesus' Birth and Growth" (*Volume 4*, Lesson 2) and the Face of "Jesus Is Lost and Found" (*Volume 4*, Lesson 3). Then add the third plaque and its story.

Notes on the Material

Find the materials for this presentation on the left of the top shelf of the Lent/Easter Shelf Unit.

The material consists of a set of seven Faces of Christ, mounted on wood plaques. The underlay is a purple and white "scroll" that unrolls to show six purple rectangles and one white rectangle made of felt. Roll up the scroll so that the white rectangle is hidden inside.

A special carrier stand for the Faces plaques stands them up, making them visible to a child scanning the room full of materials. This stand for the plaques also holds the rolled-up scroll. If you do not use this stand, put the rolled-up scroll and plaques on a tray.

Special Notes

The Faces of Easter also work well as a presentation for family storytelling around the table during Lent. A full description about how to use this lesson can be found in *Stories of God at Home: A Godly Play Approach* by Jerome Berryman. Small or mini versions of this lesson are available from Godly Play Resources, designed to be used on a table.

When told at home, instead of inviting listeners to bring other materials to the story, finish by asking special wondering questions. For example, for these first three presentations, you could ask:

- I wonder if anyone here was ever born?
- I wonder if anyone around this table was ever lost? found?
- I wonder if there is anyone in this family who was baptized?

This kind of storytelling gathers the family and its stories within the context of the Master Story of the Christian People.

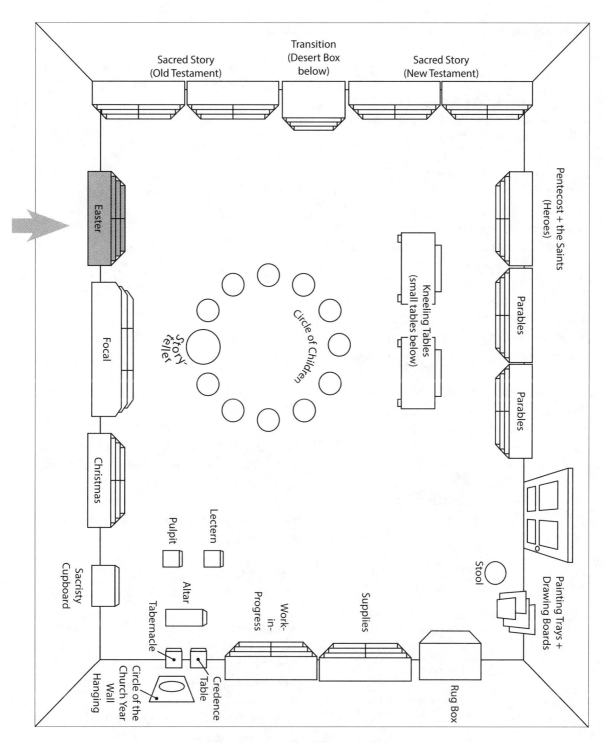

Where to Find Materials

Movements

When the children are ready, go to the Lent/ Easter Shelf Unit and bring the plaques and rolled-up scroll to the circle.

Put the plaques at your side and place the scroll in front of you. Unroll the scroll toward you to uncover the rectangle for the first plaque. Tell in summary the story "Jesus' Birth and Growth" (Volume 4, Lesson 2). When you are finished, lay down the first plaque.

Unroll the scroll to uncover the rectangle for the second section. Tell in summary the story "Jesus Is Lost and Found" (Volume 4, Lesson 3). When you are finished, lay down the second plaque.

Unroll the scroll to uncover the third rectangle. Pick up the third plaque and hold it so that the children can see it as you tell this story.

Point to John. All you can see is his hair.

Cover Jesus' face with one of your hands. Remove your hand.

Words

Watch carefully where I go so you will always know where to find this lesson.

Jesus grew and became a man. When he was about thirty years old, he went to the River Jordan, where his cousin, John, was baptizing people.

Do you see John? You can just see the back of his head. He was a wild man!

Jesus waded into the river until he was face to face with John. He said, "Baptize me."

John looked at Jesus as if for the first time. Now he saw who he really was. "How can I baptize you? You are the Messiah, the One we have been waiting for. You must baptize me."

"No. It is written that you will come before me and prepare the way. Baptize me."

Jesus went down into the darkness and chaos of the water.

Movements	**Words**

Words

When John lifted him back up into the light, there were people there who said they saw a dove come down from heaven and come close to him.

Trace the outline of the dove at the top of the plaque.

There were also people there that day who heard a voice. The voice said, "This is my beloved son, with whom I am well pleased."

After Jesus was baptized, he went on across the River Jordan into the desert. He stayed there for forty days and forty nights to learn more about who he was and what his work was going to be.

Put the third plaque down on the third rectangle of the scroll, with the face of Jesus toward the children.

Now I wonder what there is in this room that can help us tell more of the story. Look around and see if you see something. I will go around the circle and invite each one of you to go and get something to put by the pictures to help us show more of the story.

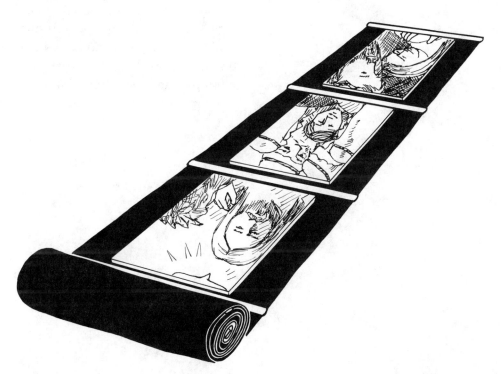

The First, Second, and Third Plaques on the Underlay (Storyteller's Perspective)

Movements

Begin to go around the circle, asking each child if he or she would like to bring something to put by the plaque illustrating "Jesus' Baptism and Blessing by God" or one of the previous plaques. Some children may not be able to think of anything, so move on if it looks as if they are stuck. You can come back to them later. If they are still stuck, that is okay. Many children learn by watching as well as by doing.

Enjoy the items that the children bring to help tell more of the story. When you have had time to enjoy the entire layout, invite children, one at a time, to return their materials. Put the plaques back on the stand in reverse order, naming each one as you do (Jesus' Birth and Growth, The Boy Lost and Found, etc.). Then take the plaques and scroll back to the Lent/Easter Shelf Unit.

Return to your spot in the circle and begin to help the children begin to get out their work.

Words

I wonder what your work will be today? You might make something about this story, or another story that you know. Maybe you want to work on something else. There are so many things you can choose from. Only you know what is right for you.

The Faces of Easter IV

Jesus' Desert and Discovery Experience
(Matthew 4:1–11; Mark 1:12; Luke 4:1–13)

How to Use This Lesson

- Core Presentation
- Liturgical Action Lesson: Lessons about sacraments or traditions of the church, which primarily use ritual and symbol to make meaning.
- As the fifth lesson in Volume 4 of *The Complete Guide to Godly Play*, it is usually presented during the season of Lent. It is part of a series of lessons meant to be told over the course of the entire season of Lent.
- It is part of a comprehensive approach to Christian formation that consists of eight volumes. Together the lessons form a spiral curriculum that enables children to move into adolescence with an inner working knowledge of the classical Christian language system to sustain them all their lives.

The Material

- Location: Lent/Easter Shelf Unit
- Pieces: Seven plaques illustrated with Faces of Christ, stand or tray
- Underlay: A strip of felt consisting of seven purple segments and one white segment. The underlay is rolled with the white on the inside.

Background

Lent is the season when we prepare for Easter. This lesson continues to help children prepare for the Mystery of Easter. We move toward the Mystery by hearing the stories of Christ's journey toward the cross and resurrection. This week's presentation focuses on Christ's temptations in the desert.

Begin this week's presentation by presenting a summary of the first three plaques:

- Jesus' Birth and Growth (*Volume 4*, Lesson 2)
- Jesus Is Lost and Found (*Volume 4*, Lesson 3)
- Jesus' Baptism and Blessing by God (*Volume 4*, Lesson 4)

Then add the fourth plaque and its story.

Notes on the Material

Find the materials for this presentation on the left of the top shelf of the Lent/Easter Shelf Unit.

The material consists of a set of seven Faces of Christ, mounted on wood plaques. The underlay is a purple and white "scroll" that unrolls to show six purple rectangles and one white rectangle. Roll up the scroll so that the white rectangle is hidden inside.

A special carrier stand for the Faces plaques stands them up, making them visible to a child scanning the room full of materials. This stand for the plaques also holds the rolled-up scroll. If you do not use this stand, put the rolled-up scroll and plaques on a tray.

Special Notes

Inviting children to bring materials to put next to the stories introduces a technique of "side-by-side" connections. Bringing a story or object from the shelves to another story is one way to extend or enrich a lesson. In addition, you can tell two Godly Play stories together and invite children to make their own links. This works especially well with older children. For example, you could tell the creation story (see *The Complete Guide to Godly Play, Volume 2*, Lesson 4) side-by-side with the Faces stories. Ask children, for example, "I wonder where this day (from the Creation) belongs in this story (the Faces)?"

Sometimes Godly Play mentors enjoy this type of wondering so much they are tempted to introduce it with every story. We suggest that you limit this so it does not become stale or rote.

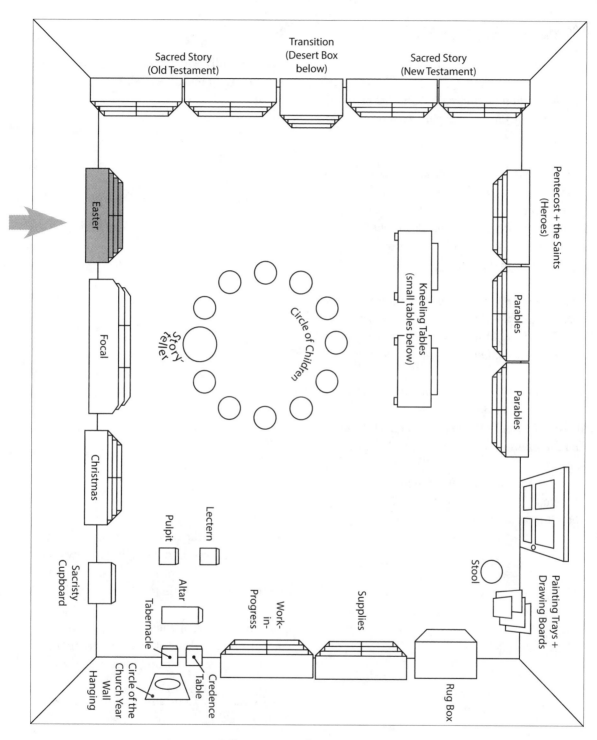

Where to Find Materials

Movements

When the children are ready, go to the Lent/Easter Shelf Unit and bring the plaques and rolled-up scroll to the circle.

Put the plaques at your side and place the scroll in front of you. Unroll the scroll toward you to uncover the rectangle for the first plaque. Tell in summary the story "Jesus' Birth and Growth" (Volume 4, Lesson 2). When you are finished, lay down the first plaque.

Unroll the scroll to uncover the rectangle for the second plaque. Tell in summary the story "Jesus Is Lost and Found" (Volume 4, Lesson 3). When you are finished, lay down the second plaque.

Unroll the scroll to uncover the third rectangle. Tell in summary the story "Jesus' Baptism and Blessing by God" (Volume 4, Lesson 4). When you are finished, lay down the third plaque.

Unroll the scroll to uncover the fourth section. Pick up the fourth plaque and hold it so that the children can see it as you tell this story.

Words

Watch carefully where I go so you will always know where to find this lesson.

Jesus went into the desert to discover more about who he was and what his work was going to be. He was there for forty days and forty nights. There was little to eat or to drink.

One day he heard a voice. It said, "Why don't you turn one of those stones over there into bread and have something to eat?"

Jesus said, "No. To be a real human being, we need more than just bread to eat."

Suddenly, it was as if Jesus were on top of the great Temple in Jerusalem. The voice came back, "If you are really the Son of God, why don't you jump and see if God sends the angels to catch you before you hit the stones below?"

Movements	Words
	Jesus said, "No. We do not need to test God."
	Then, it was as if Jesus could see all the kingdoms of the world. The voice came back again: "If you will follow me, I will make you king over all these kingdoms."
	Jesus said, "No. I am to be a king, but not that kind of king."
	Then the voice went away.
	Jesus went back across the River Jordan and began to do his work.
Put the fourth plaque down on the fourth rectangle of the scroll.	
	Now I wonder what there is in this room that can help us tell more of the story. Look around and see if you find something. I will go around the circle and invite each one of you to go and get something to put by the pictures to help us show more of the story.

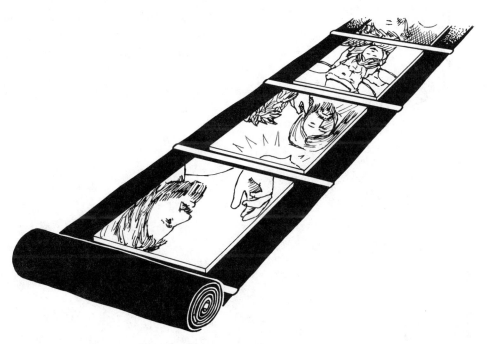

The Second, Third, and Fourth Plaques on the Underlay (Storyteller's Perspective)

Movements

Begin to go around the circle, asking each child if he or she would like to bring something to put by the plaque illustrating "Jesus' Desert and Discovery Experience" or one of the previous plaques. Some children may not be able to think of anything, so move on if it looks as if they are stuck. You can come back to them later. If they are still stuck, that is okay. Many children learn by watching as well as by doing.

Enjoy the items that the children bring to help tell the story. When you have had time to enjoy the entire layout, invite children, one at a time, to return their materials. Put the plaques back on the stand in reverse order, naming each one as you do (Jesus' Birth and Growth, The Boy Lost and Found, etc.). Then take the plaques and scroll back to the Lent/Easter Shelf Unit.

Return to your spot in the circle and begin to help the children begin to get out their work.

Words

I wonder what your work will be today? You might make something about this story, or another story that you know. Maybe you want to work on something else. There are so many things you can choose from. Only you know what is right for you.

Lesson 6

The Faces of Easter V

*Jesus as Healer and Parable-Maker
(Matthew 4:23, Matthew 13:1–35;
Mark 1:32–34; Mark 4:1–34; Luke 4:38–44;
Luke 8:4–15; John 5:1–18; John 10:1–42, and
many more!)*

How to Use This Lesson

- Core Presentation
- Liturgical Action Lesson: Lessons about sacraments or traditions of the church, which primarily use ritual and symbol to make meaning.
- As the sixth lesson in Volume 4 of *The Complete Guide to Godly Play*, it is usually presented during the season of Lent. It is part of a series of lessons meant to be told over the course of the entire season of Lent.
- It is part of a comprehensive approach to Christian formation that consists of eight volumes. Together the lessons form a spiral curriculum that enables children to move into adolescence with an inner working knowledge of the classical Christian language system to sustain them all their lives.

The Material

- Location: Lent/Easter Shelf Unit
- Pieces: Seven plaques illustrated with Faces of Christ, stand or tray
- Underlay: A strip of felt consisting of seven purple segments and one white segment. The underlay is rolled with the white on the inside.

Background

Lent is the season when we prepare for Easter. This lesson continues to help children prepare for the Mystery of Easter. We move toward the Mystery by hearing the stories of Christ's journey toward the cross and resurrection. This week's presentation focuses on the face of Christ as healer and Parable-maker.

Begin this week's presentation by presenting a summary of the first four plaques:

- Jesus' Birth and Growth (*Volume 4*, Lesson 2)
- Jesus Is Lost and Found (*Volume 4*, Lesson 3)
- Jesus' Baptism and Blessing by God (*Volume 4*, Lesson 4)
- Jesus' Desert and Discovery Experience (*Volume 4*, Lesson 5)

Then add the fifth plaque and its story.

Notes on the Material

Find the materials for this presentation on the left of the top shelf of the Lent/Easter Shelf Unit.

The material consists of a set of seven Faces of Christ, mounted on wood plaques. The underlay is a purple and white "scroll" that unrolls to show six purple rectangles and one white rectangle. Roll up the scroll so that the white rectangle is hidden inside.

A special carrier stand for the Faces plaques stands them up, making them visible to a child scanning the room full of materials. This stand for the plaques also holds the rolled-up scroll. If you do not use this stand, put the rolled-up scroll and plaques on a tray.

Special Notes

When Jerome Berryman first developed the presentations of the Faces of Christ, he thought it might be suitable only for older children. However, teachers at Christ Cathedral in Houston, who worked with these materials, used them with younger children, too—children as young as two years old. For the youngest children, keep the stories short, especially the summaries of previous stories. When you summarize the stories for very young children, you might only use a sentence or two for each story, for example:

- Here is the baby who was born.
- Here is the boy who was lost and found.

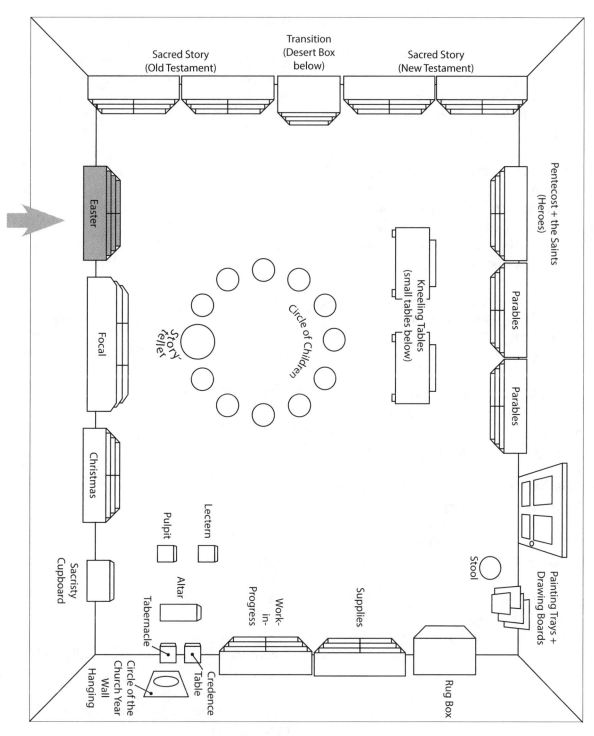

Where to Find Materials

Sacred Story (Old Testament)

Transition (Desert Box below)

Sacred Story (New Testament)

Easter

Focal

Christmas

Sacristy Cupboard

Pulpit

Lectern

Altar

Tabernacle

Work-in-Progress

Supplies

Circle of the Church Year Wall Hanging

Credence Table

Story-teller

Circle of Children

Kneeling Tables (small tables below)

Pentecost + the Saints (Heroes)

Parables

Parables

Stool

Painting Trays + Drawing Boards

Rug Box

Movements

When the children are ready, go to the Lent/ Easter Shelf Unit and bring the plaques and rolled-up scroll to the circle.

Put the plaques at your side and place the scroll in front of you. Unroll the scroll toward you to uncover the rectangle for the first plaque. Tell in summary the story "Jesus' Birth and Growth" (Volume 4, Lesson 2). When you are finished, lay down the first plaque.

Unroll the scroll to uncover the rectangle for the second plaque. Tell in summary the story "Jesus Is Lost and Found" (Volume 4, Lesson 3). When you are finished, lay down the second plaque.

Unroll the scroll to uncover the third rectangle. Tell in summary the story "Jesus' Baptism and Blessing by God" (Volume 4, Lesson 4) When you are finished, lay down the third plaque.

Unroll the scroll to uncover the fourth rectangle. Tell in summary the story "Jesus' Desert and Discovery Experience" (Volume 4, Lesson 5). When you are finished, lay down the fourth plaque.

Unroll the scroll to uncover the fifth rectangle. Pick up the fifth plaque and hold it so that the children can see it as you tell this story.

Words

Watch carefully where I go so you will always know where to find this lesson.

Jesus came back across the River Jordan and began to do his work . . . but what was his work? His work was to come close to people, especially the people no one else wanted to come close to.

See? He has come close to this blind man; he is so close that he has touched the blind man's eyes.

Movements

Point to the blind man.

Put the fifth plaque down on the fifth rectangle of the scroll.

Words

When Jesus came close to people, they changed. They could see things they had never seen before. They could do things they had never done before. They became well.

Jesus also told Parables. Finally, he knew that he had to become a Parable, so he turned toward Jerusalem for the last time.

Now I wonder what there is in this room that can help us tell more of the story. Look around and see if you can bring something to show more about this story. I will go around the circle and invite each one of you to go and get something to put by the pictures to help us show more of the story.

The Third, Fourth, and Fifth Plaques on the Underlay (Storyteller's Perspective)

Movements

Begin to go around the circle, asking each child if he or she would like to bring something to put by the plaque illustrating "Jesus as Healer and Parable-Maker" or one of the previous plaques. Some children may not be able to think of anything, so move on if it looks as if they are stuck. You can come back to them later. If they are still stuck, that is okay. Many children learn by watching as well as by doing.

Enjoy the items that the children bring to help tell the story. When you have had time to enjoy the entire layout, invite children, one at a time, to return their materials. Put the plaques back on the stand in reverse order, naming each one as you do (Jesus' Birth and Growth, The Boy Lost and Found, etc.). Then take the plaques and scroll back to the Lent/Easter Shelf Unit.

Return to your spot in the circle and begin to help the children begin to get out their work.

Words

I wonder what your work will be today? You might make something about this story, or another story that you know. Maybe you want to work on something else. There are so many things you can choose from. Only you know what is right for you.

The Faces of Easter VI

Jesus Offers the Bread and Wine
(Matthew 26:17–29; Mark 12:12–16; Luke 22:7–13)

How to Use This Lesson

- Core Presentation
- Liturgical Action Lesson: Lessons about sacraments or traditions of the church, which primarily use ritual and symbol to make meaning.
- As the seventh lesson in Volume 4 of *The Complete Guide to Godly Play*, it is usually presented during the season of Lent. It is part of a series of lessons meant to be told over the course of the entire season of Lent.
- It is part of a comprehensive approach to Christian formation that consists of eight volumes. Together the lessons form a spiral curriculum that enables children to move into adolescence with an inner working knowledge of the classical Christian language system to sustain them all their lives.

The Material

- Location: Lent/Easter Shelf Unit
- Pieces: Seven plaques illustrated with Faces of Christ, stand or tray
- Underlay: A strip of felt consisting of seven purple segments and one white segment. The underlay is rolled with the white on the inside.

Background

Lent is the season when we prepare for Easter. This lesson continues to help children prepare for the Mystery of Easter. We move toward the Mystery by hearing the stories of Christ's journey toward the cross and resurrection. This week's presentation focuses on the face of Christ as he enters Jerusalem and offers the Twelve—and us—the bread and wine.

Begin this week's presentation by presenting a summary of the first five plaques:

- Jesus' Birth and Growth (*Volume 4*, Lesson 2)
- Jesus Is Lost and Found (*Volume 4*, Lesson 3)
- Jesus' Baptism and Blessing by God (*Volume 4*, Lesson 4)
- Jesus' Desert and Discovery Experience (*Volume 4*, Lesson 5)
- Jesus as Healer and Parable-Maker (*Volume 4*, Lesson 6)

Then add the sixth plaque and its story.

Notes on the Material

Find the materials for this presentation on the left of the top shelf of the Lent/Easter Shelf Unit.

The material consists of a set of seven Faces of Christ, mounted on wood plaques. The underlay is a purple and white "scroll" that unrolls to show six purple rectangles and one white rectangle. Roll up the scroll so that the white rectangle is hidden inside.

A special carrier stand for the Faces plaques stands them up, making them visible to a child scanning the room full of materials. This stand for the plaques also holds the rolled-up scroll. If you do not use this stand, put the rolled-up scroll and plaques on a tray.

Special Notes

If you do not have Godly Play on Easter Sunday proper you will want to go on and tell the next lesson about Good Friday and Easter Sunday (Lesson 8). Alternatively you could use Lesson 8 at a gathering during Holy Week.

At Home: A full description about how to use this series of lessons at home can be found in *Stories of God at Home: A Godly Play Approach* by Jerome Berryman. Small or mini versions of this lesson are available from Godly Play Resources, designed to be used on a table. When telling these stories in a home setting, substitute "I wonder" questions for the activity of bringing other materials to place beside the plaques. Suitable "I wonder" questions for the last four Faces stories include:

- I wonder if anybody around this table has discovered who they are and what their work is going to be?
- I wonder if anyone in this family has come close to people—especially people no one else wanted to come close to? I wonder if anyone here has told parables? I wonder if anyone around this table has ever been sick?
- I wonder if anyone here has come close to holy bread and wine?
- I wonder if anyone here remembers their very best Easter? I wonder what the earliest Easter is you can remember?

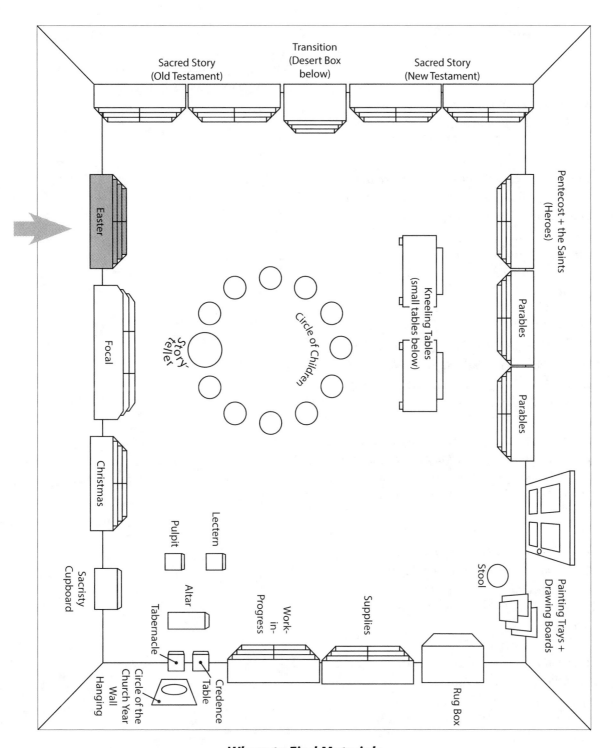

Where to Find Materials

Movements

When the children are ready, go to the Lent/ Easter Shelf Unit and bring the plaques and rolled-up scroll to the circle.

Put the plaques at your side and place the scroll in front of you. Unroll the scroll toward you to uncover the rectangle for the first plaque. Tell in summary the story "Jesus' Birth and Growth" (Volume 4, Lesson 2). When you are finished, lay down the first plaque.

Unroll the scroll to uncover the rectangle for the second section. Tell in summary the story "Jesus Is Lost and Found" (Volume 4, Lesson 3). When you are finished, lay down the second plaque.

Unroll the scroll to uncover the third rectangle. Tell in summary the story "Jesus' Baptism and Blessing by God" (Volume 4, Lesson 4). When you are finished, lay down the third plaque.

Unroll the scroll to uncover the fourth section. Tell in summary the story "Jesus' Desert and Discovery Experience" (Volume 4, Lesson 5). When you are finished, lay down the fourth plaque.

Unroll the scroll to uncover the rectangle for the fifth plaque. Tell in summary the story "Jesus as Healer and Parable-Maker" (Volume 4, Lesson 6). When you are finished, lay down the fifth plaque.

Unroll the scroll to uncover the sixth section. Pick up the sixth plaque and hold it so that the children can see it as you tell this story.

Words

Watch carefully where I go so you will always know where to find this lesson.

Movements

Words

Jesus went to Jerusalem for the last time. It was the time of the Passover, so the city was full of people from many different lands. They thought Jesus was coming to be king, but they weren't paying attention.

He wasn't riding a great white horse like a king. He wasn't being carried by soldiers. He was riding on a donkey, and it wasn't even his. He had to borrow it.

Still that Sunday when Jesus came into Jerusalem, people waved palm branches, which were a sign of kings.

On Monday, Tuesday, and Wednesday, Jesus went into the Temple to teach. Every night he went back to the Mount of Olives with the Twelve. The people watched him and whispered that the Mount of Olives was where angels were supposed to come down to make an army to drive away the Roman soldiers.

You might skip this part of the story for younger children and pick up with "The Temple Guards . . ." below.

Optional Section

One day when Jesus was teaching in the Temple, he said, "Do you see that old woman over there? She's going to put something in the money box. Listen. Did you hear anything? No. She put the smallest coin there is in the box. That is all the money she has.

Now, here comes a rich man. He has so much money to put into the money box that he needs help to carry it. Listen. The money clangs and rings as they pour it into the box.

Now, I wonder which one really gave the most, the old woman or the rich man."

Some said the rich man gave the most. Some said the old woman.

End Optional Section

Movements	Words
	The Temple guards said, "On Thursday we will take Jesus." But on Thursday, they could not find him. That evening, Jesus and the Twelve hurried through the dark streets to a house. They climbed up the stairs to an upper room and shared their last supper together.
	After they had everything they wanted to eat, Jesus took some bread and gave thanks to God for it. Then he broke it and said something like, "Whenever you break the bread like this and share it, I will be there." He also took a cup of wine, gave thanks to God for it, and said, "Whenever you share a cup of wine like this, I will be there."
Point to the bread and the wine as you mention them.	
	What was he talking about? He was always saying things like that. How could they know? Still, they did not forget, and later they would understand.
	Suddenly, Judas, one of the Twelve, got up and left. The rest sang a hymn and then went to the Garden of Gethsemane on the Mount of Olives. Jesus wanted to pray. When he was finished, he joined the Twelve, but Judas came out of the dark and greeted him with a kiss on the cheek.
Touch the side of Jesus' face.	This was a signal for the Temple guards to take him. They came out of the shadows and took Jesus away with them into the night. The Twelve also disappeared into the darkness.
	Now, I wonder what there is in this room that can help us tell more of the story. Look around and see if you see something you can bring to put beside these pictures. I will go around the circle and invite each one of you to go and get something to put by the pictures to help us show more of the story.

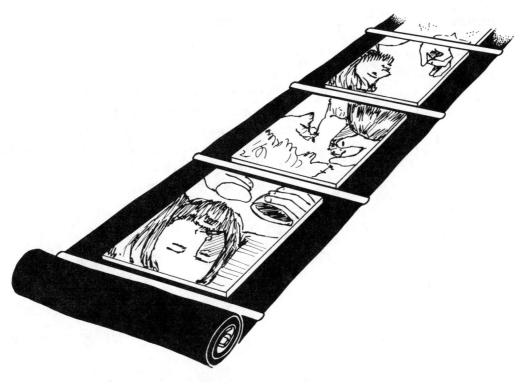

The Fourth, Fifth, and Sixth Plaques on the Underlay (Storyteller's Perspective)

Movements	Words

Begin to go around the circle, asking each child if he or she would like to bring something to put by the plaque illustrating "Jesus Offers the Bread and Wine" or one of the other plaques. Some children may not be able to think of anything, so move on if it looks as if they are stuck. You can come back to them later. If they are still stuck, that is okay. Many children learn by watching as well as by doing.

Enjoy the items that the children bring to help tell the story. When you have had time to enjoy the entire layout, invite children, one at a time, to return their materials. Put the plaques back on the stand in reverse order, naming each one as you do (Jesus' Birth and Growth, The Boy Lost and Found, etc.). Then take the plaques and scroll back to the Lent/Easter Shelf Unit.

Movements

Return to your spot in the circle and begin to help the children get out their work.

Words

I wonder what your work will be today? You might make something about this story, or another story that you know. Maybe you want to work on something else. There are so many things you can choose from. Only you know what is right for you.

Lesson 8

The Faces of Easter VII

The One Who Was Easter and Still Is
(Matthew 26:30–28:10; Mark 14:26–16:8;
Luke 22:39–24:12; John 18:1–20:31)

How to Use This Lesson

- Core Presentation
- Liturgical Action Lesson: Lessons about sacraments or traditions of the church, which primarily use ritual and symbol to make meaning.
- As the eighth lesson in Volume 4 of *The Complete Guide to Godly Play*, it is usually presented during the season of Lent. It is part of a series of lessons meant to be told over the course of the entire season of Lent.
- It is part of a comprehensive approach to Christian formation that consists of eight volumes. Together the lessons form a spiral curriculum that enables children to move into adolescence with an inner working knowledge of the classical Christian language system to sustain them all their lives.

The Material

- Location: Lent/Easter Shelf Unit
- Pieces: Seven plaques illustrated with Faces of Christ, stand or tray
- Underlay: A strip of felt consisting of seven purple segments and one white segment. The underlay is rolled with the white on the inside.

Background

Lent is the season when we prepare for Easter. This lesson continues to help children prepare for the Mystery of Easter. We move toward the Mystery by hearing the stories of Christ's journey toward the cross and resurrection. This last presentation focuses on the Faces of Christ on the cross and on Easter.

Begin this week's presentation by presenting a summary of the first six plaques:

- Jesus' Birth and Growth (*Volume 4*, Lesson 2)
- Jesus Is Lost and Found (*Volume 4*, Lesson 3)
- Jesus' Baptism and Blessing by God (*Volume 4*, Lesson 4)
- Jesus' Desert and Discovery Experience (*Volume 4*, Lesson 5)
- Jesus as Healer and Parable-Maker (*Volume 4*, Lesson 6)
- Jesus Offers the Bread and Wine (*Volume 4*, Lesson 7)

Then add the last plaque and its story.

Notes on the Material

Find the materials for this presentation on the left of the top shelf of the Lent/Easter Shelf Unit.

The material consists of a set of seven Faces of Christ, mounted on wood plaques. The underlay is a purple and white "scroll" that unrolls to show six purple rectangles and one white rectangle. Roll up the scroll so that the white rectangle is hidden inside.

A special carrier stand for the Faces plaques stands them up, making them visible to a child scanning the room full of materials. This stand for the plaques also holds the rolled-up scroll. If you do not use this stand, put the rolled-up scroll and plaques on a tray.

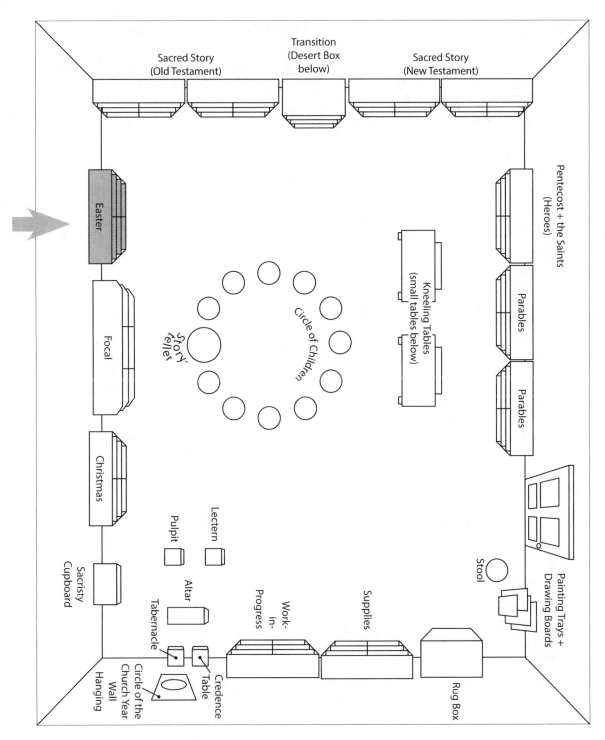

Sacred Story
(Old Testament)

Transition
(Desert Box
below)

Sacred Story
(New Testament)

Pentecost + the Saints
(Heroes)

Easter

Focal

Kneeling Tables
(small tables below)

Parables

Circle of Children

Story-
teller

Parables

Christmas

Lectern

Pulpit

Stool

Painting Trays +
Drawing Boards

Sacristy
Cupboard

Altar

Tabernacle

Work-
in-
Progress

Supplies

Rug Box

Circle of the
Church Year
Wall
Hanging

Credence
Table

Where to Find Materials

Movements

When the children are ready, go to the Lent/ Easter Shelf Unit and bring the plaques and rolled-up scroll to the circle. Put the plaques at your side and place the scroll in front of you. Unroll the scroll toward you to uncover the rectangle for the first plaque. Tell in summary the story "Jesus' Birth and Growth" (Volume 4, Lesson 2). When you are finished, lay down the first plaque.

Unroll the scroll to uncover the rectangle for the second section. Tell in summary the story "Jesus Is Lost and Found" (Volume 4, Lesson 3). When you are finished, lay down the second plaque.

Unroll the scroll to uncover the third rectangle. Tell in summary the story "Jesus' Baptism and Blessing by God" (Volume 4, Lesson 4). When you are finished, lay down the third plaque.

Unroll the scroll to uncover the fourth section. Tell in summary the story "Jesus' Desert and Discovery Experience" (Volume 4, Lesson 5). When you are finished, lay down the fourth plaque.

Unroll the scroll to uncover the rectangle for the fifth plaque. Tell in summary the story "Jesus as Healer and Parable-Maker" (Volume 4, Lesson 6). When you are finished, lay down the fifth plaque.

Unroll the scroll to uncover the rectangle for the sixth plaque. Tell in summary the story "Jesus Offers the Bread and Wine (Volume 4, Lesson 7). When you are finished, lay down the sixth plaque.

Words

Watch carefully where I go so you will always know where to find this lesson.

Movements

Don't unroll the seventh section of the scroll yet. Pick up the seventh plaque and hold it, with the face of Christ on the cross facing the children. Tell this story:

Point to the dark sky.

Turn the plaque slowly here; point to the bread and wine.

Turn the plaque slowly back and forth as you describe the Faces in this part of the story, showing first one side, then the other. Finally, turn the edge of the plaque toward the children and "try" to pull the two sides apart.

Now unroll the white rectangle of the scroll.

Words

The night was long and confusing. The next day, Jesus was taken outside the walls of the city and crucified.

That afternoon, Jesus died. The sky grew dark.

Jesus was taken down from the cross and buried in a cave. A great stone was rolled into the opening of the cave to close it like a door.

Saturday was so quiet you could almost hear the earth breathing. On Sunday, it was the women who had the courage to go to the tomb just to be close to Jesus. They wanted to remember everything, even if it was sad. When they came to the tomb, they found that the stone had been rolled away. When they looked inside the tomb was empty.

Jesus had died on the cross, but somehow he was still with them as he is with us, especially in the bread and the wine.

When you look at this side *(crucifixion)* you know that the other side is there *(Easter)*. When you look at this side *(Easter)*, you know that this side *(crucifixion)* is there, and you cannot pull them apart.

This is the Mystery of Easter, and that makes all the difference . . .

Movements

Put the seventh plaque down on the white rectangle, with the face of the Risen Christ facing up.

Words

. . . and so the color changes from purple to white—the color of pure celebration.

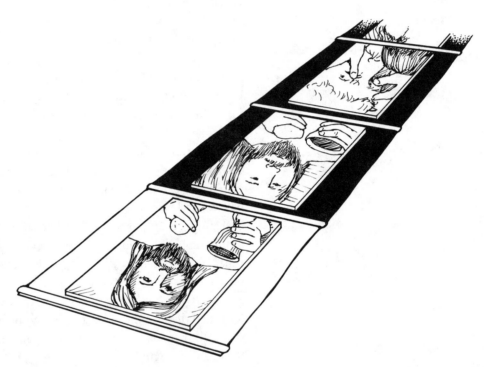

The Fifth, Sixth, and Seventh Plaques on the Underlay (Storyteller's Perspective)

Sit back and enjoy the complete story laid out in a line, then look puzzled. Say:

Wait a minute. There's something wrong.

Here's the beginning . . . the middle . . . and the end.

Point to each part as you call attention to the linear layout of the story.

Movements

Pick up the seventh plaque and turn it to the crucifixion side.

Turn the plaque over to the Easter side and show it to the children.

Put the Easter plaque back on the white panel, resurrection side up.

Pick up the first plaque and roll the scroll toward you, out of the way. Place the first plaque down where the first portion of the scroll was.

Pick up the second plaque and roll up the second section of the scroll. Place the second plaque where indicated on the illustration that follows.

Pick up the third plaque and roll up the third section of the scroll. Place the third plaque where indicated in the illustration.

Pick up the fourth plaque and roll up the fourth section of the scroll. Place the fourth plaque where indicated in the illustration.

Pick up the fifth plaque and roll up the fifth section of the scroll. Place the fifth plaque where indicated in the illustration.

Pick up the sixth plaque and roll up the sixth section of the scroll. Place the sixth plaque where indicated in the illustration.

Words

Look! If we have only this side, the story has an end . . .

. . . but there is also this side.

The ending is also a beginning, so we can't leave the story in a line.

Let's see what we can do.

Movements

Words

Finally, pick up the seventh plaque and hold it while you finish rolling up the scroll. Place the scroll beside you. Place the seventh plaque (resurrection side up) in the middle of the layout where indicated in the illustration.

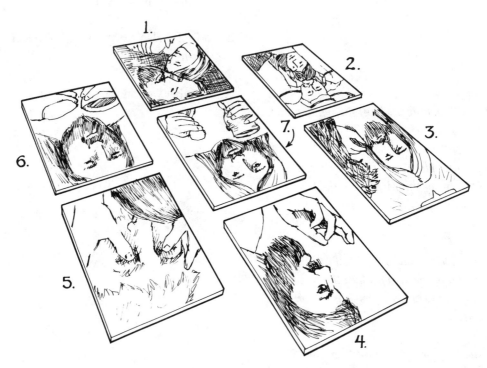

The Circle of Faces (Storyteller's Perspective)

Now the story can go on forever.

Sit back and reflect silently for a moment.

Then begin the wondering.

I wonder what part of this story you like best?

I wonder what part of the story is the most important part?

I wonder where you are in this story? What part of the story is about you?

Movements

When the energy in the wondering begins to wane, put the plaques back on the stand in reverse order. Name each one as you put them on the stand (Jesus' Birth and Growth, Jesus is Lost and Found, etc.). Finally take the plaques and scroll back to the Lent/Easter Shelf Unit.

Then return to your spot in the circle and begin to help the children make choices about the work they are going to get out.

Be sure to reroll the underlay later, beginning with the white panel so it will be in position for the next use.

Words

I wonder if there is any part of the story we can leave out and still have all the story we need?

I wonder what your work will be today? You might make something about this story, or another story that you know. Maybe you want to work on something else. There are so many things you can choose from. Only you know what is right for you.

The Crosses

Exploring a Sacred Symbol

How to Use This Lesson

- Enrichment Lesson
- Liturgical Action Lesson: Lessons about sacraments or traditions of the church, which primarily use ritual and symbol to make meaning.
- As the ninth lesson in Volume 4 of *The Complete Guide to Godly Play* it can be presented at any time of the year, but is especially appropriate when a child announces he or she is going to make a cross during response time.
- It is part of a comprehensive approach to Christian formation that consists of eight volumes. Together the lessons form a spiral curriculum that enables children to move into adolescence with an inner working knowledge of the classical Christian language system to sustain them all their lives.

The Material

- Location: Lent/Easter Shelf Unit
- Pieces: Collections of crosses in a container; cards to name and explain the crosses
- Underlay: Use a plain rug or felt underlay

Background

Save this lesson for the time when a child decides to "make a cross" for his or her art response. It's great fun to hold this in reserve for such an occasion, because when a child says, "I'm going to make a cross," you can say, "Which one?"

This lesson is also useful when a child cannot think of anything at all to make, even "a cross." You can get the basket of crosses and begin to wonder with him or her about what they all mean and who first made them. This can lead to the child making a cross that is just right for his or her life.

The cross lesson can be started quickly and put away quickly. It can take as long as the child wants to work on it. You can present this to an individual child, without introducing it through a group lesson.

Notes on the Material

Find the materials for this presentation on the right-hand side of the bottom shelf of the Lent/Easter Shelf Unit, underneath the material for the Legend of the Easter Egg presentation (*Volume 4*, Lesson 10).

There are several ways to make this material. You could simply put all the three-dimensional, wooden crosses you collect into a basket and place it on the shelf. You could also draw or mount cross shapes on cards or wooden plaques, and create an additional set of cards with stories or explanations about each cross.

The best material combines the two approaches. In a beautiful container, place a set of wooden cross shapes. Make a set of cards with the names of each cross shape and an explanation of that shape to serve as identification and control cards for the children. (Control cards help children sort the material and make sure each item is present and named.) The collection offered through Godly Play Resources includes a Greek cross, a Latin cross, a Celtic cross, a budded cross, a St. Andrew's cross, an Egyptian (or Coptic) cross, and an anchor cross.

Special Notes

Sometimes children make crosses because they can't think of anything else to make. If so, they might not go very deeply into the activity, because they are doing it for you and not out of personal interest. This lesson challenges them to think about what crosses really represent and how to work with crosses to find the cross that is just right for them. This can reveal important things about who they are or hope to be.

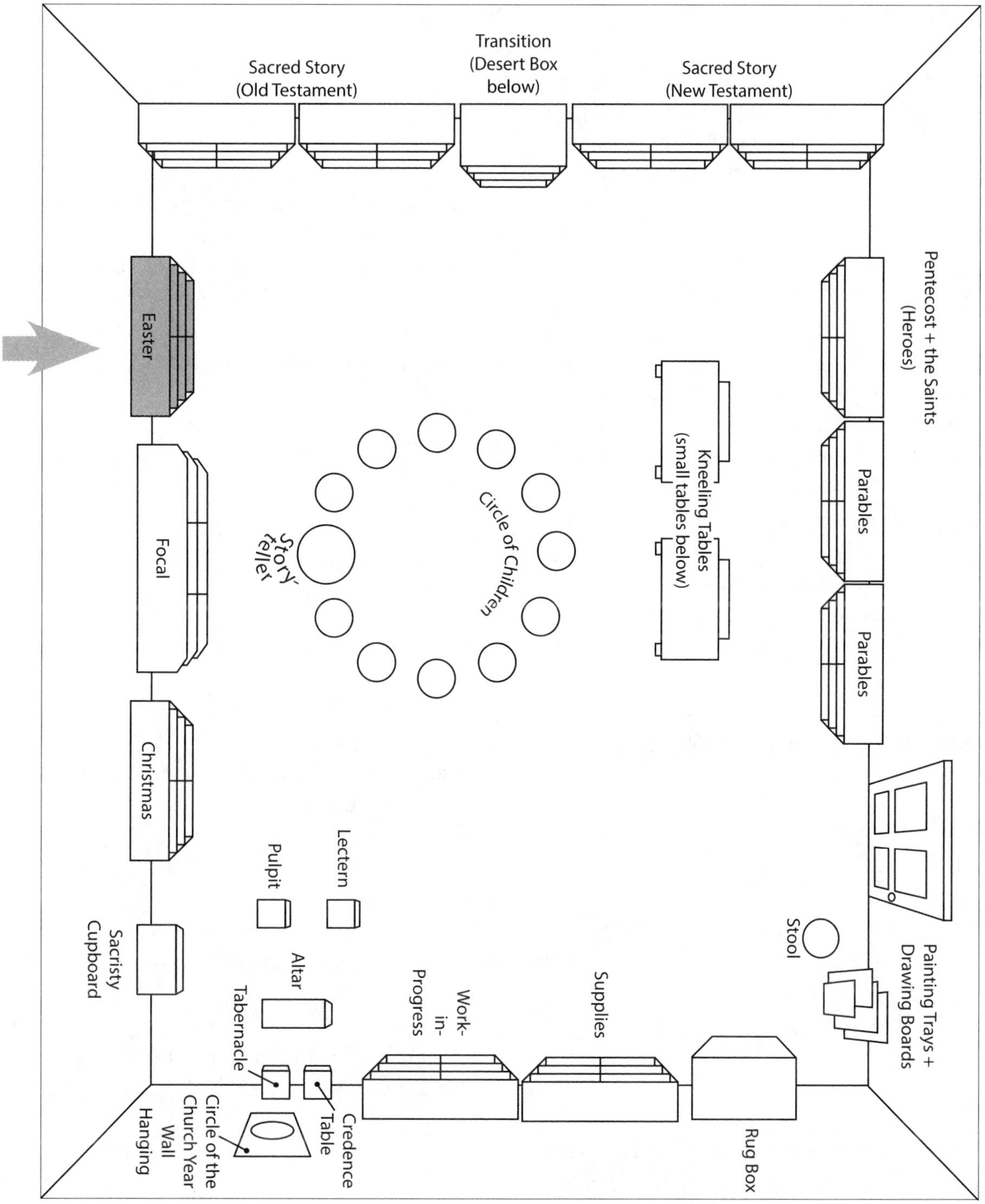
Sacred Story
(Old Testament)
Transition
(Desert Box
below)
Sacred Story
(New Testament)
Easter
Focal
Christmas
Sacristy
Cupboard
Pentecost + the Saints
(Heroes)
Parables
Parables
Kneeling Tables
(small tables below)
Circle of Children
Story-
teller
Lectern
Pulpit
Altar
Tabernacle
Credence
Table
Circle of the
Church Year
Wall
Hanging
Work-
in-
Progress
Supplies
Rug Box
Stool
Painting Trays +
Drawing Boards

Where to Find Materials

Movements

When children cannot decide what to do, or when then say they are going to "make a cross," you can challenge them to discover more about crosses and about themselves.

Don't say too much about where the crosses in the room or container of crosses might be. This can help a child or group search the room and become more familiar with all the materials that are there waiting for them to work with.

As the children look, go and get a rug. Spread it out in just the right place. Then, if necessary, go find the basket of crosses.

Bring the basket back to the rug. Take out the crosses and line them up on the rug.

If there is a set of cards to use as a control, you can explain them to the children. Show the pictures of the crosses and the names for and explanations about them. Read them for the nonreaders.

Words

Oh, so you would like to make a cross? That will be wonderful work. Let's see now . . . which one are you going to make? There are so many kinds! How many? Oh, I don't know, but there are many in our room. Why don't you see if you can find them? The cross helps us remember the Mystery of Easter.

Look at all these crosses. Do you see the differences between them?

Would you like to make one? Which one would you like to make?

What will you make it out of? Do you want to draw or paint one?

Can you make one that is different from any in the basket? Can you make one that is just right for you?

These cards are for you. You can use them when you have questions or when you want to name the crosses.

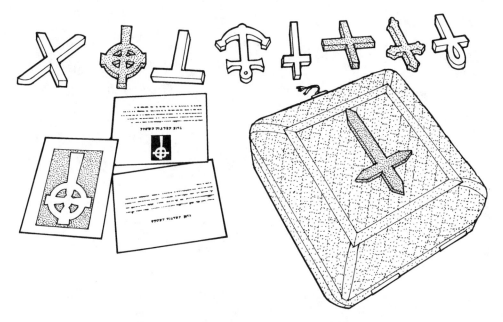

The Crosses (Storyteller's Perspective)

Movements

Begin the wondering questions.

Put the crosses back into the container for the children to work with. As you put them back hold them carefully and with respect.

Don't hurry. Name each cross with wonder as you replace it.

Words

Now I wonder which cross you like best?

I wonder which is the most important cross?

I wonder which cross is especially for you?

I wonder if we can leave out any of these crosses and still have all the crosses we need?

Now I wonder if you would like to make something about how these crosses feel to you?

Lesson 10

The Legend of the Easter Eggs

Symbols of the Mystery of Easter

How to Use This Lesson

- Enrichment Lesson
- Liturgical Action Lesson: Lessons about sacraments or traditions of the church, which primarily use ritual and symbol to make meaning.
- As the tenth lesson in Volume 4 of *The Complete Guide to Godly Play* it is usually presented during the season of Easter.
- It is part of a comprehensive approach to Christian formation that consists of eight volumes. Together the lessons form a spiral curriculum that enables children to move into adolescence with an inner working knowledge of the classical Christian language system to sustain them all their lives.

The Material

- Location: Lent/Easter Shelf Unit
- Pieces: One large wooden tray (big enough to hold all the materials listed), one smaller wooden tray holding one to three Ukrainian Easter eggs in translucent boxes; one real (or wooden) egg in a small basket covered with a white cloth; collection of two-dimensional, egg-shaped samples of colors, designs and finished patterns; a control card that explains the meaning of the patterns, shapes, and colors
- Underlay: Use a plain rug or felt underlay

Background

The folk celebration of Easter eggs brings delight at this time of year. In many places Easter eggs have little to do with the Easter that is celebrated in churches, but the eggs of Eastern Europe do. Introducing children to these eggs is a way to reclaim a wonderful sign of new life in Easter for children.

The story you will tell in this lesson is a legend, but it has as its starting point something we do read about in the story of the Passion—the encounter that Jesus has on the way to the cross with a man named Simon of Cyrene who was "coming in from the country" on the day of the crucifixion (Matthew 27:32, Mark 15:21, Luke 23:26).

Notes on the Material

Find the materials for this presentation on the right-hand side of the middle shelf of the Lent/Easter Shelf Unit, underneath the material for the Synagogue and the Upper Room.

This material fits onto one large tray, about one foot by two feet (about thirty by sixty centimeters). Inside the large tray are three additional containers:

- One square tray (eight inches by eight inches or about twenty by twenty centimeters) holds up to three Ukrainian Easter eggs in translucent boxes with lids.
- A basket (six inches by six inches or about fifteen by fifteen centimeters) containing a real or wooden egg covered by a white cloth. Before beginning the presentation, take one of the Ukrainian Easter eggs out of its translucent box and place it in this basket.
- A third tray (or small basket) holds a collection of flat, egg-shaped wood or cardboard samples showing some of the traditional colors and design elements used in making Ukrainian Easter eggs.

In addition, place the control sheet in the bottom of the large tray (we recommend laminating it or placing it in a protective sleeve), showing the meaning of the colors and symbols.

Meaning of the Traditional Colors

white	purity
yellow	spirituality
blue	health
pink	success
black	remembrance
orange	attraction
brown	happiness
green	money
purple	high power
red	love

Meaning of the Traditional Design Elements

butterfly	nature
flower	love, charity
circle, poppy, spider web	the sun, good fortune
checkerboard, sieve	filtering good from evil
ladders	growing, climbing to heaven

fish	ancient Christian symbol
bends, spirals	Life doesn't always go in "straight lines."
deer, horses	prosperity, wealth
wheat	bountiful harvest
hens, roosters, sparrows, storks	wishes coming true (The birds are always resting.)
rose (traditionally looks like a star)	wisdom or guidance, beauty and elegance
cross	suffering, death, resurrection of Christ
ram's horns	strength, determination
eight-pointed star	About 988 CE, this sign of the sun god became a symbol for the Christian God.
pine trees, needles	eternal youth and health
dots	stars in heaven, Mary's tears
designs encircling the egg	eternity

Other Design Elements, Meaning Unknown

Spoons or leaves	Spoons stand alone. Leaves come in two and threes.
rake	For sorting and planting

Same Egg Patterns and Designs

It is recommended that you add a tray of materials on the Response Shelves for making Easter eggs (during the Easter season). You will need a basket of plain wooden eggs or blown out real eggs for the children to decorate. When the children have worked out a design for their egg they can get one of these eggs to decorate. If you use the wooden eggs, we recommend spray painting them white in advance, and using colored pencils to make the designs. You can also include a collection of small baskets and Easter "grass" so that when the eggs are fully decorated the child can place them in the basket and bring them home.

Special Notes

The Ukrainian eggs in the translucent boxes are real and fragile. If one gets broken, leave it in its box so the children can see for themselves how thin the shells are.

A children's book that shows real children making Ukrainian Easter eggs is *A Kid's Guide to Decorating Ukrainian Easter Eggs* by Natalie Perchyshyn (Ukrainian Gift Shop, 2000).[1]

---

1 www.ukrainiangiftshop.com (accessed July 13, 2017).

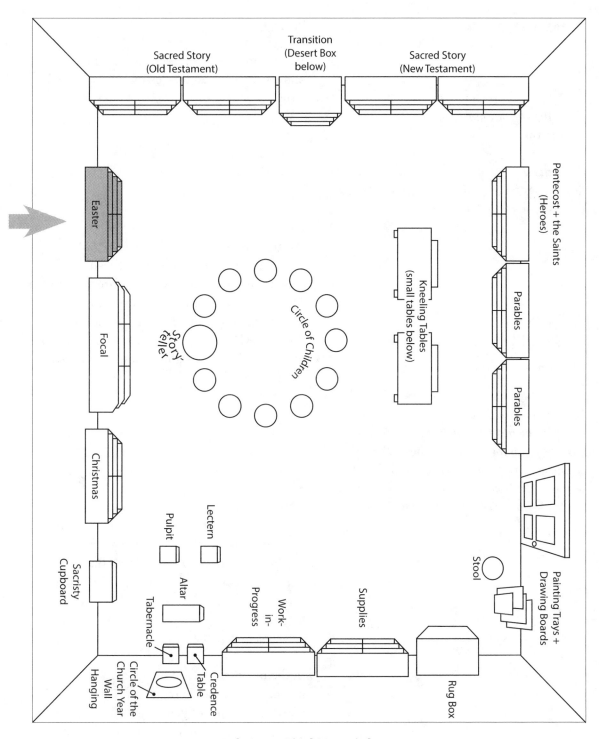

Where to Find Materials

Movements

Go to the rug box and get a rug. Unroll it in front of you.

Go to the shelves and find the materials for the Easter Eggs lesson. Place the materials beside you. When you and the children are settled, begin.

In the middle of the circle, place the six inch by six inch (about fifteen by fifteen centimeters) basket containing a covered single Ukrainian Easter egg. (You prepared this before the session.) Hold the white, real (or wooden) egg hidden in your closed hand.

Words

Watch carefully where I go so you will always know where to find this lesson. First we need a rug.

Now watch again.

We are coming close to the Mystery of Easter. There are all kinds of ways to get ready to come close to this great mystery. Some are done in the church, and some are done outside the church. One of the things done outside of the church is to make Easter eggs. The only trouble is that many people have forgotten how to make real Easter eggs. They don't even know their story. Let me tell you the story.

There was once an old man and an old woman who lived just outside the walls of the great city of Jerusalem. They had everything they needed. They had a cow to give them milk. They had a garden to give them vegetables. They had trees to give them apples, figs, and dates. They had chickens to give them eggs.

In the morning the old man would go out to the hen house and say to the hens, "Good morning. May I have some of your eggs?" They gladly gave him their eggs, and there were plenty. There were so many on some days that the old man took the ones they did not eat into the city to sell.

Movements

Turn your hand over and show the children the white egg. Put the egg in the basket. As you do so, keep the Ukrainian egg hidden under the cover. Put the basket down in front of you.

Words

One day he went into the great city of Jerusalem with a basket full of eggs. A white cloth covered them. He went in through a high gate and went along a narrow stone street. As he came closer to one of the wide streets, there was a huge crowd. They were strangely quiet. He pushed his way through the crowd with his basket of eggs to see what was going on.

The Roman soldiers were taking three people through the city to crucify them outside the city walls. They were carrying the crosses they were to be nailed to. One of them stumbled and almost fell as the old man watched.

He couldn't help it. He stepped out from the crowd and caught the heavy, wooden beam before the man fell. The soldiers made him carry the piece of wood as he followed Jesus outside the walls.

The old man stayed there all afternoon, even when the sky grew dark and it began to rain. He watched the Mother Mary and others standing there as Jesus suffered and died.

They took Jesus down and carried him away to put in a stone tomb. The old man did not follow. He started back toward home. He suddenly remembered his eggs. Where were they?

He hurried back to where he had begun to carry the cross. He wondered if they would be there?

Movements

Take out the colored egg.

Pick up the basket so the children can't see inside.

When the story is finished, return the Ukrainian egg you've been using to its box and take out the other Ukrainian eggs. Place all three eggs, in their boxes, on the rug. Show the eggs to the children.

Show children the egg shapes with samples of traditional colors and design elements. Lay them out in lines as you describe them.

Words

He turned the corner, and like a joke, looked at the place he had put down the basket. It was there! He rubbed his eyes. He looked again. Yes. It was really there.

He looked in the basket. The white covering was still there, but he knew the eggs underneath would be gone. He reached under the white cover. There was something there.

When he pulled out one of the eggs, he could not believe his eyes. It was like a jewel!

The old man picked up the basket and pulled back the cover. The basket was full of beautiful eggs. They were covered with colors and designs. The eggs were trying to say with colors and lines what had happened that day!

When the old man told this story, people began to color eggs at Eastertime, and they still do to this very day. Some don't even know why, but you do.

Here are shapes of eggs you can trace to fill in with your own design. Here are colors and designs that other people have used, but there is no one else in the world who knows what your egg is supposed to look like. Only you can decide.

Movements	Words
	Here is how you can make a booklet about your egg.
Fold an eight and one-half inch by eleven inch (twenty-two by twenty-eight centimeters) sheet of paper in half and then fold that half in half again to make a booklet.	
	On the cover of your booklet, you can draw an egg shape.
Trace an egg shape on the front of the cover with your finger.	
	Decorate your drawing of an egg. Look up what everything means. Write that on the inside of your booklet.
Show them the control that says what everything stands for.	
If you are planning to have children decorate real eggs, either wooden or fresh, you can say:	
	When you are finished with the booklet, you can then decorate an egg.
If you are supplying wooden eggs, you can say:	These eggs were not laid by chickens, but they are "forest fresh." They come from trees.
	When the egg is finished, we will put it in a basket with grass so you can give it to anyone, even to yourself.
If you do not have baskets prepared you can just invite the children to take the decorated egg home.	
Begin the wondering questions.	
	Now I wonder which of the colors and designs you like best?
	I wonder which colors and designs are the most important?
	I wonder which colors and designs are especially about you?

Movements

Take your time putting everything back on the tray.

Return the materials to the shelves. Then return to your spot in the circle so you can begin to help the children choose their work.

Words

I wonder if these are all the designs and colors we need? Maybe we need more? Are there too many? Not enough?

Now watch carefully how I put this all away. That way you will know how to do it if you make this your work.

Now, watch where I go to put it on the shelves.

I wonder what your work will be today? You might make something about this story, or another story that you know. Maybe you want to decorate an egg? Maybe you want to work on something else? There are so many things you can choose from. Only you know what is right for you.

Lesson 11

Jesus and the Twelve

The Disciples who became Apostles
(Matthew 10:2–4; Matthew 26:21;
Mark 3:16–19; Mark 14:18; Luke 6:14–16;
Luke 22:21; John 13:21; Acts 1:2; & 13)

How to Use This Lesson

- Core Presentation
- Sacred Story: The stories of how God and people meet.
- As the eleventh lesson in Volume 4 of *The Complete Guide to Godly Play* it is usually presented before the Day of Pentecost.
- It is part of a comprehensive approach to Christian formation that consists of eight volumes. Together the lessons form a spiral curriculum that enables children to move into adolescence with an inner working knowledge of the classical Christian language system to sustain them all their lives.

The Material

- Location: Sacred Story (New Testament) Shelves
- Pieces: Picture of Last Supper, symbols for the Twelve Apostles, control card
- Underlay: None

Background

This presentation is called "Jesus and the Twelve" to avoid calling the Twelve either disciples or apostles. There are four lists of the apostles in the New Testament, found in Matthew 10:2–4, Mark 3:16–19, Luke 6:14–16, and Acts 1:2 and 13. The four lists give contradictory names for the Twelve. This historical difficulty has several scholarly solutions, but our pedagogical purpose is to present the group as the Twelve, with a fixed set of names.

We will use this list, based on the traditional names for the Twelve, together with their traditional symbols:

Name	Symbol
Andrew	white X-shaped cross on blue background
Bartholomew	three knives
James (son of Zebedee)	three scallop shells and often a sword
James the Less (son of Alphaeus)	saw
John	cup and serpent
Jude	sailboat
Matthew	three money bags
Philip	cross with two loaves of bread
Thomas	builder's square and spear
Simon Peter	upside down cross and crossed keys
Simon, the Zealot	book and fish

These eleven apostles exclude Judas because he removed himself through his betrayal and suicide. The twelfth shield is for Matthias, who replaced Judas after Jesus' ascension into heaven. His symbol is the sword and a book.

Notes on the Material

Find the materials for this presentation on the top shelf of the Sacred Story Shelves, next to the Greatest Parable (*Volume 8*, Lessons 1–4). The lesson uses a reproduction of Da Vinci's *The Last Supper*, which leans against the wall in the New Testament section. In front of the painting, there should be a tray holding a small basket or wood container containing twelve small shields and a control card (described below).

Godly Play Resources provides a simplified painting of the scene found in Da Vinci's painting, mounted on wood. However, you can also purchase a poster reproduction of the actual painting and get it mounted on foam core. The moment Da Vinci depicts is the reaction of the disciples to Christ's statement that one of the disciples is "about to betray me" (Matthew 26:21; Mark 14:18; John 13:21; Luke 22:21). The palm of Jesus' left hand is turned up, as if to say, "Not my will but thine be done," or to call attention to the bread. The palm of his other hand is turned down and has more tension as if to suppress his anxiety (John 13:21).

Some notes on the painting which you may want to discuss with older children:

- The people are dressed in the clothes of the painter's time and place. They are late fifteenth-century, north Italian and wealthy. The painting was painted 1495–1498 about the time Columbus discovered America (1492).
- They look like someone who might buy a painting from Da Vinci.
- A more important cultural issue is the painting's display of anti-Semitism. The only person who looks "Jewish," dark with curly hair, is Judas. Children will remind you that they have Jewish friends, however, who don't look like that. For his time, Da Vinci painted a representative figure, a stereotype.
- *The Last Supper* is a late fifteenth-century mural painting (not a fresco) by Leonardo da Vinci in the refectory of the Convent of Santa Maria delle Grazie, Milan. It is one of the world's most famous paintings.
- This is only one artist's idea of what the Last Supper might have looked like. We recommend that you have other versions in your Godly Play room. A Polish artist named Bohdan Piasecki paints one that includes women and children, in a Jewish setting.

As you tell the story, you will place each shield above the head of the matching apostle. A small version of the painting is used as a control card to identify each apostle. This can be used as a control for children who work with this lesson on their own, but is also helpful for the storyteller. Another control card is included in this lesson that shows pictures of the shields with the names and brief stories of the matching apostles.

Matching Shields to Apostles (Storyteller's Perspective)

Special Notes

In telling this story, you can change the order of presenting the Twelve from the one we give in order to tell the stories of those apostles whose symbols and stories you remember first, hoping the others will come to mind as you proceed. The lesson uses the four groupings of three apostles as suggested by the Da Vinci painting.

Additional significant groups are:

- two sets of brothers: Peter and Andrew, James and John (sons of Zebedee)
- the inner circle, present at the Transfiguration: Peter, James, and John
- one set of friends: Philip and Bartholomew
- those directly called by Jesus: Philip and Matthew
- the only one to die a natural death: John

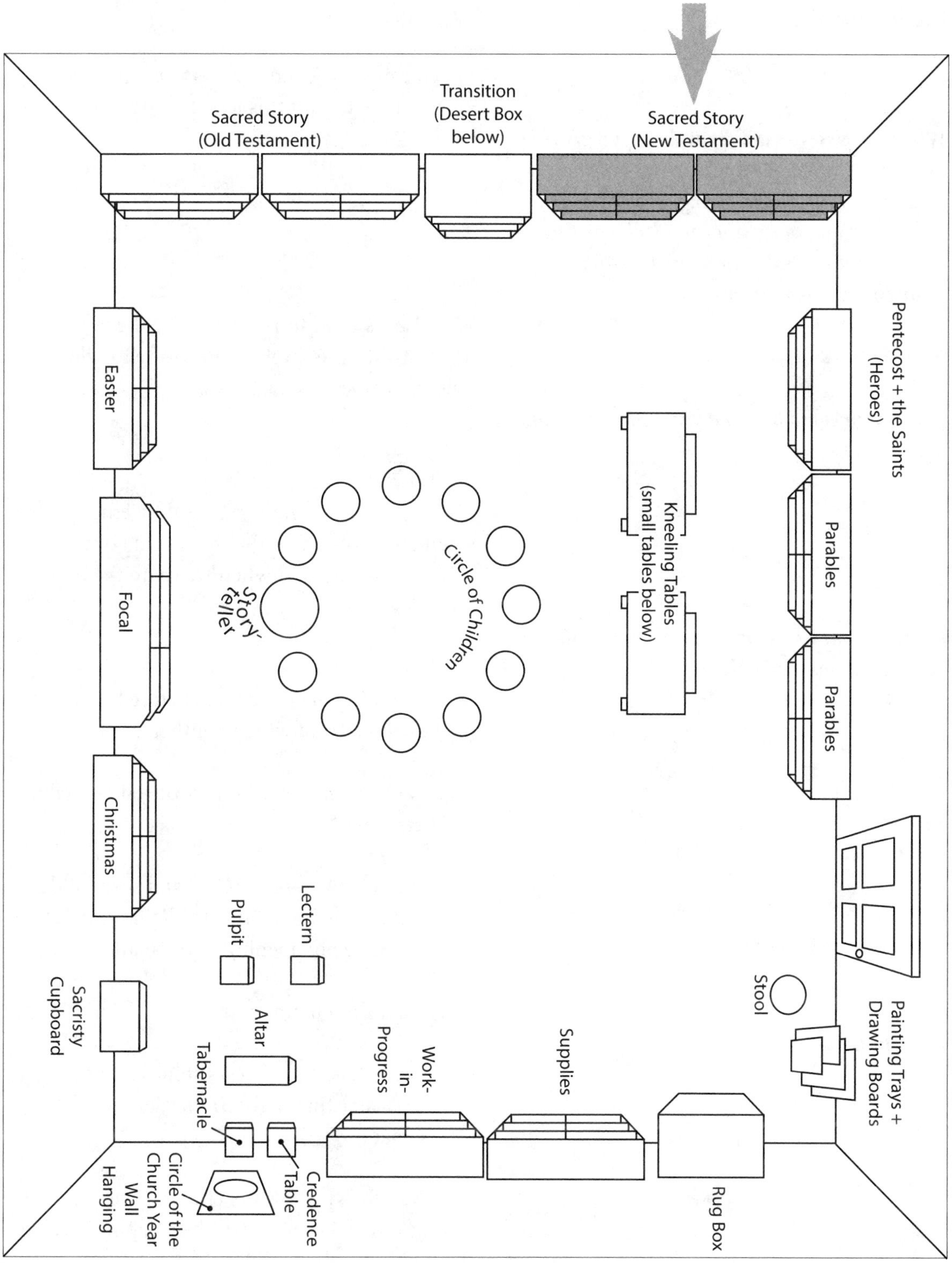

Sacred Story
(Old Testament)
Transition
(Desert Box
below)
Sacred Story
(New Testament)
Easter
Focal
Christmas
Sacristy
Cupboard
Pentecost + the Saints
(Heroes)
Parables
Parables
Kneeling Tables
(small tables below)
Circle of Children
Story-
teller
Lectern
Pulpit
Altar
Tabernacle
Credence
Table
Circle of the
Church Year
Wall
Hanging
Work-
in-
Progress
Supplies
Rug Box
Stool
Painting Trays +
Drawing Boards

Where to Find Materials

Movements

When the children are ready, bring the picture and tray of materials to the circle. Put the picture in front of you, facing away from you. As you tell this story, you can tilt the picture up, laying it against your knees to help the children see it more clearly.

Sweep your hand over the picture as you name the Twelve.

Point to some of the bread and wine on the table when you name them.

Point to Jesus.

Point to Judas.

Take the shields from their container and lay them across the top of the picture in random order.

Words

Watch carefully where I go so you will always know where to find this lesson.

When Jesus went to Jerusalem for the last time, he went with the Twelve. They were his closest followers called the disciples.

On Thursday of the last week, they met in an upstairs room for their last meal together. It was when Jesus told them that he would always be with them—and us—when we share the holy bread and wine.

But something happened just before he shared the holy bread and wine with them.

Jesus said, "Someone who is sitting at this table will betray me."

All the disciples were shocked and sorry and angry. They cried out, "Is it I?" "Who is it?" That is what you see happening in the painting.

Later, Judas did betray Jesus.

He showed the High Priest's soldiers who Jesus was later that night in the Garden of Gethsemane.

These are the symbols the church gave the disciples after they began to tell the story and became apostles.

Movements

Use your finger to draw an imaginary circle around each one of the groups.

Point to John. With the picture facing away from you toward the children, John is seated directly to your right of Jesus.

Move the shield for John down from the row of shields along the top of the picture so that it rests right over his head.

Lean back and pause each time before moving on to the next apostle. Now point to Peter. With the picture facing away from you toward the children, Peter is seated directly to the right of John, two places to the right from Jesus and behind Judas as you look at the picture.

Words

Each one has a special sign to help us remember them and their stories.

Jesus is in the middle. The disciples are in groups of three on either side. Let's see who's here.

This is John. He is probably the one called the "beloved disciple." John first learned about Jesus when he was with John the Baptist. Right away he told his brother, James, and they both began to follow Jesus. Both brothers were fishermen. Their father's name was Zebedee. John is probably the one who wrote down the story of Jesus we call "The Gospel of John."

This is the symbol for John.

On his shield are the cup and the snake. They help us remember how one time some people tried to put poison into his cup, but the snake came and drank it. The snake died to save John's life.

Stories say that John was the only apostle who was not killed. He died on an island when he was an old man, full of years.

This is Peter. He is leaning in toward Jesus behind Judas. Peter often got angry. He looks angry now, but he became more peaceful as the years went by.

Movements

Move the shield for Peter down from the row of shields along the top of the picture so that it rests right over his head.

Point to Judas. With the picture facing away from you toward the children, Judas is seated to the right and in front of Peter, three places to the right of Jesus.

Move the blank shield for Judas down over his head. There is no symbol for Judas.

Words

Peter heard about Jesus from his brother, Andrew, who was with John the Baptist. He is sitting next to his brother, but it is hard to tell because of the way he is leaning in toward John. The two brothers look a lot alike.

Peter's sign is the crossed keys and an upside-down cross. One time Jesus said to Peter that he was the rock on which he would build the church. He then said that he gave Peter the keys to the kingdom.

When Peter was old, he went to be with the Christian people in Rome. It was against the law to be a Christian person in those days, and the soldiers caught him. When they were going to nail him to a cross like Jesus, Peter asked them to turn him upside down. He did not deserve to die like his Lord, he said. The soldiers did as he asked, and old Peter died on the cross, too, but upside down.

Judas is the one who turned against Jesus. See? He is holding a bag with thirty pieces of silver in the painting. That is what he was paid to show the soldiers who Jesus was when they went to arrest him in the Garden of Gethsemane.

I wonder what symbol would be best for Judas?

Sometimes the sign for Judas is a shield that is all black, but I wonder if there was really no light in his life at all? Sometimes the sign for Judas also has the thirty pieces of silver or a rope on it because Judas hanged himself when he realized what he had done. Judas may have lost hope for himself, but I wonder if Jesus forgave him?

Movements

Put the blank shield on the tray. Then move the shield for Matthias down from the row of shields along the top of the picture, over the head of Judas.

Draw an imaginary circle around the next group of three, the three closest to the other side of Jesus.

Point to Thomas. With the picture facing away from you toward the children, Thomas is seated to the left of Jesus, behind James.

Move the shield for Thomas down from the row of shields along the top of the picture so that it rests right over his head.

Point to James. With the picture facing away from you toward the children, James is seated to the left of Jesus, in front of Thomas. Show how James is really sitting next to Jesus, even though the face of Thomas is closer to Jesus.

Words

Perhaps it's best to simply leave his shield blank.

This is the sign for Matthias. He replaced Judas as one of the Twelve and was killed for telling the story, so his symbol is a kind of sword and a book.

On the other side of Jesus are Thomas, James, and Philip.

This is Thomas. He is leaning behind James, so we see his face next to Jesus, even though James is really sitting next to Jesus. Thomas was the one who always asked hard questions. He is sometimes called "doubting Thomas."

His sign is a spear and a builder's square. This is what a builder uses to make square corners on buildings. Thomas went to India to tell people the story of Jesus, so he began to build the Church in that part of the world. He was killed in India for telling the story.

This is James. He is really sitting next to Jesus. His brother, John, is on one side, and he is on the other. He and his brother were fishermen, like Peter and Andrew. They worked for their father, Zebedee.

Movements

Words

James learned about Jesus from his brother, John, who learned about him when he was a disciple of John the Baptist. The two brothers, John and James, together with Peter, made up an inner circle of three very close friends of Jesus inside the group of the Twelve. The three were there when Jesus was praying on the mountain and when he was praying in the garden, but I'm afraid they went to sleep three times in the garden.

Move the shield for James down from the row of shields along the top of the picture so that it rests right over his head.

The sign for James is three shells. He was the first apostle to be killed. King Herod Agrippa the First had him executed. This is why a sword is also sometimes on his symbol.

Point to Philip. With the picture facing away from you toward the children, Philip is seated to the left of James, three places to the left of Jesus. Trace how Philip is leaning in toward Jesus.

Philip is next. He was there when Jesus fed the five thousand people. They were hungry for the truth about life. The truth is that people need each other and need to love each other. To show this, Jesus shared a little bread and fish with them and there was enough for all. It was kind of like a Parable.

Move the shield for Philip down from the row of shields along the top of the picture so that it rests right over his head.

His sign has two loaves of bread on it to remember that day when so many were fed so well.

Move your finger across to the other end of the table, the right side of the table with the picture facing away from you toward the children. Then circle the group of three disciples there.

Now we will go back to the other side, clear to the end of the table. Here there is another group of three people. They are Andrew, James the Less, and Bartholomew.

Movements	Words
Point to Andrew. With the picture facing away from you toward the children, Andrew is seated to the right of Judas, four places to the right of Jesus.	Here is Andrew. We already know he is Peter's brother. See how he is sitting near Peter? Andrew was one of John the Baptist's disciples, but when John the Baptist showed Jesus to him, he went to get his brother Peter, and they both followed Jesus. Both Andrew and Peter were fishermen.

Movements

Point to Andrew. With the picture facing away from you toward the children, Andrew is seated to the right of Judas, four places to the right of Jesus.

Move the shield for Andrew down from the row of shields along the top of the picture so that it rests right over his head.

Point to James the Less. With the picture facing away from you toward the children, James the Less is seated to the right of Andrew, five places to the right of Jesus.

Move the shield for James the Less down from the row of shields along the top of the picture so that it rests right over his head.

Point to Bartholomew. With the picture facing away from you toward the children, Bartholomew is seated at the farthest right of the table.

Words

Here is Andrew. We already know he is Peter's brother. See how he is sitting near Peter? Andrew was one of John the Baptist's disciples, but when John the Baptist showed Jesus to him, he went to get his brother Peter, and they both followed Jesus. Both Andrew and Peter were fishermen.

Many centuries ago the people of Scotland liked Andrew so much that they made him the patron saint of Scotland.

If you should ever go there, you will still see his sign, the cross that looks like an "X." He died on a cross that was this shape.

James the Less is next. People called him "the Less" because he was younger or shorter than John's brother James.

James the Less' sign is a saw. He was killed by a saw for telling the story of Jesus. Kings did not like to hear about following "a king" called Jesus, even though Jesus was a different kind of king.

Finally at this end of the table we come to Bartholomew. His name means "Son of Tolmai." He was told about Jesus by Philip after Jesus told Philip to follow him.

Movements

Move the shield for Bartholomew down from the row of shields along the top of the picture so that it rests right over his head.

Move your finger across to the other end of the table, the left side of the table with the picture facing away from you toward the children. Then circle the group of three disciples there.

Point to Matthew. With the picture facing away from you toward the children, Matthew is seated to the left of Philip, four places to the left of Jesus.

Move the shield for Matthew down from the row of shields along the top of the picture so that it rests right over his head.

Point to Jude. With the picture facing away from you toward the children, Jude is seated to the left of Matthew, five places to the left of Jesus.

Move the shield for Jude down from the row of shields along the top of the picture so that it rests right over his head.

Words

This is Bartholomew's sign. He was killed by knives for telling the story of Jesus by people who did not understand.

At the other end of the table is the last group of three. They are Matthew, Jude, and Simon the Zealot.

Here is Matthew. He was a tax collector from Capernaum until Jesus called him. Matthew followed Jesus and later wrote down the story of Jesus we call "The Gospel of Matthew." It is the first book in the New Testament.

Here is Matthew's symbol. It has three money bags on it to help us remember that he was a hated tax collector before Jesus called him and Matthew found peace.

This is Jude. His name almost sounds like "Judas." He may have written the next-to-last book in the New Testament, which is a letter by Jude.

His symbol is a ship sailing, because he went across the sea to tell the story of Jesus.

Movements

Point to Simon. With the picture facing away from you toward the children, Simon is seated at the farthest left of the table.

Move the shield for Simon down from the row of shields along the top of the picture so that it rests right over his head.

Sit back and pause a little longer than after each apostle's presentation.

Sweep your hand across all the apostles and then return to touch the shield above each head.

When the wondering subsides, you can take a moment to point out that the painting of the Last Supper you are using is just one artist's idea of what it might have looked like. Many artists have tried to draw this scene. It is recommended that you have a few different versions of the Last Supper in your room. You can even go and get them off the shelf and compare them with Da Vinci's version.

Words

Here is Simon. He was a fighter for his people and for God's law so he was called "the Zealot." He was also a fisherman.

The symbol of Simon is a fish and a book. The fish helps us remember that he was a fisherman who became someone who fished for people to show them the truth about life. The book stands for the Bible.

These are the Twelve, the Apostles, and these are their symbols.

Now, I wonder which one of the Twelve you like best?

I wonder which one was the most important?

I wonder which one is most like you? Where are you in this story?

I wonder if we can leave any of the Twelve out and still have all of the story that we need?

Movements

Now put the material away and begin to help the children decide what work they are going to get out.

Words

I wonder what your work will be today? You might make something about this story, or another story that you know. Maybe you want to work on something else. There are so many things you can choose from. Only you know what is right for you.

Lesson 12

The Good Shepherd and World Communion[2]

The Good Shepherd and Holy Communion
(John 10:1–18; Psalm 23)

How to Use This Lesson

- Core Presentation
- Liturgical Action Lesson: Lessons about sacraments or traditions of the church, which primarily use ritual and symbol to make meaning.
- As the twelfth lesson in Volume 4 of *The Complete Guide to Godly Play*, it can be presented any Sunday in the church year.
- It is part of a comprehensive approach to Christian formation that consists of eight volumes. Together the lessons form a spiral curriculum that enables children to move into adolescence with an inner working knowledge of the classical Christian language system to sustain them all their lives.

The Material

- Location: Focal Shelf Unit
- Pieces: Good Shepherd, sheep, sheepfold, table, priest (or minister), people of the world, small container holding a paten and chalice
- Underlay: Two circles made of wood (about twelve inches diameter or about thirty centimeters) covered in green felt

Background

This lesson places the image of the Good Shepherd from John 10 and Psalm 23 beside Holy Communion. The images of the Good Shepherd and Holy Communion deepen each other's interpretation when set side-by-side like this. One does not need to step outside the domain of religious language into the language of philosophy or science, for example, to talk

---

2 This lesson was suggested by the work of Sofia Cavelletti. The reader should be aware, however, that both the teaching material and the lesson are substantially changed and put to a different use in Godly Play than in her work. Please see Jerome Berryman's *The Spiritual Guidance of Children* (2013), which explores the relationship between Montessori and Cavelletti in Chapters 2 and 3, for further information.

about the two religious images or interpret them. One can remain *within* religious language, meditating, while the images disclose the depths in each other.

Notes on the Material

In an ideal setup, the Focal Shelf Unit is the shelf unit directly opposite the door the children enter. The Holy Family sits in the center of the top shelf. To the right of the Holy Family as you face the shelf unit is one green circle (the circle is made of wood and is covered with green felt) with the figure of the Good Shepherd, the sheepfold, and his sheep. Place the shepherd in the opening of the sheepfold so that he is "the gate" of the sheepfold (John 10:7 and 10:9). The sheepfold is a set of hinged wooden fence pieces. On the shelf below the Good Shepherd and his sheep, there is another green circle (just like the one on the top shelf) with a table standing at its center. On the shelf below the second circle, there is a basket that holds a priest or minister, the people of the world, and a small container. The container holds a paten and chalice to represent the bread and wine.

Special Notes

As you can see, this is a Liturgical Action Lesson, which interprets the Christian tradition of communion. It is not included among the Parable lessons, because Parables function in a different way than liturgical action, although there is always some overlap. This presentation does tell a story, but it is not part of the Sacred Story materials because it focuses on the liturgical action and the symbols by which that action carries its meaning to us and to which we respond.

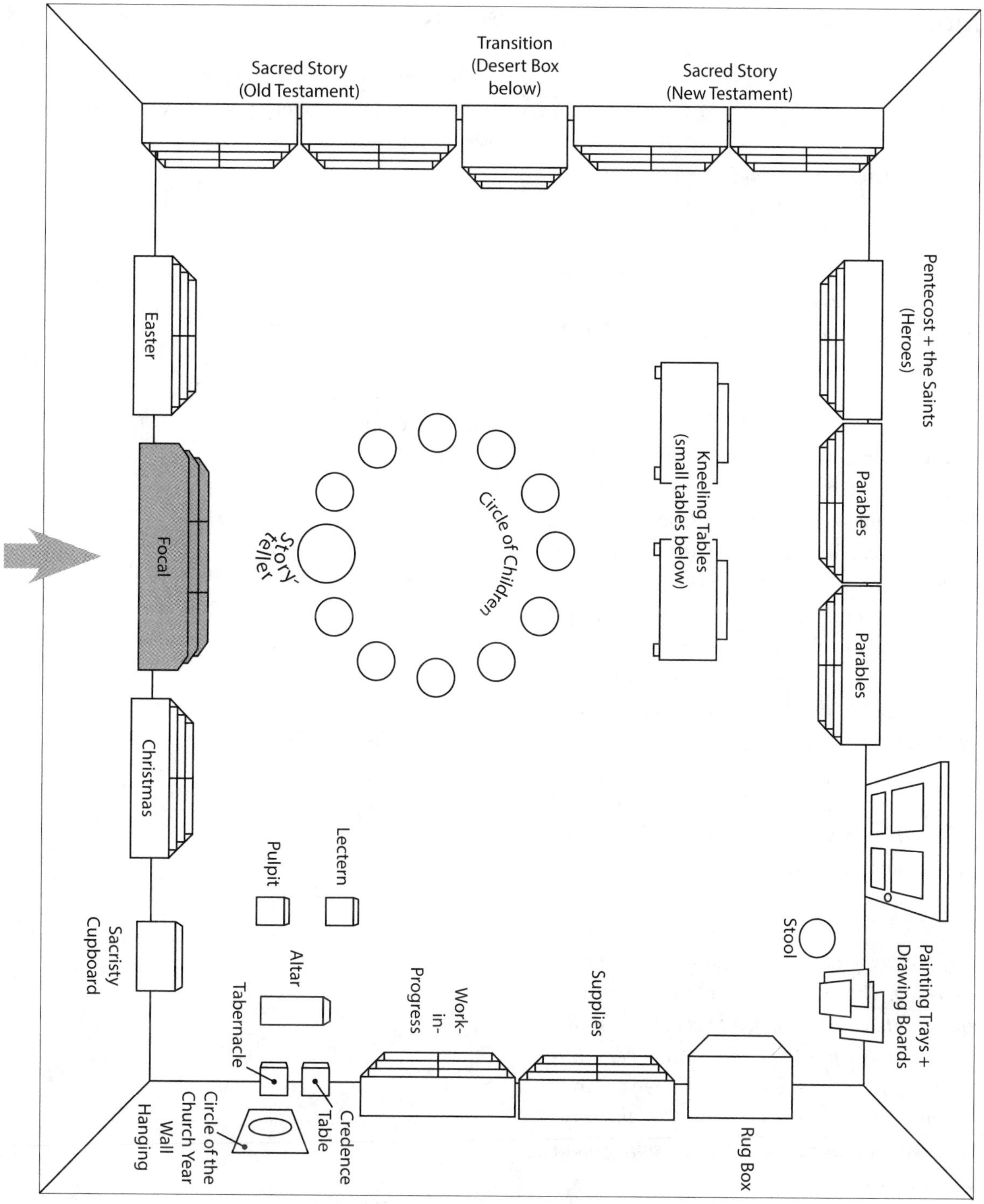
Sacred Story
(Old Testament)
Transition
(Desert Box
below)
Sacred Story
(New Testament)
Easter
Focal
Christmas
Sacristy
Cupboard
Pentecost + the Saints
(Heroes)
Parables
Parables
Kneeling Tables
(small tables below)
Circle of Children
Story
teller
Lectern
Pulpit
Altar
Tabernacle
Credence
Table
Circle of the
Church Year
Wall
Hanging
Work-
in-
Progress
Supplies
Rug Box
Stool
Painting Trays +
Drawing Boards

Where to Find Materials

Movements

Even though the material is right behind you, on the Focal Shelf Unit, get up and walk around the circle to find the material. This is much more dramatic than merely reaching out to pull the pieces off the shelves. The children will gain a better sense of where the material is kept.

Carry the material carefully, with two hands, as you want the children to carry it. First bring the green circle with the Good Shepherd, the sheepfold, and the sheep to the storytelling circle. We recommend laying the Good Shepherd down on the green circle before picking it up so he doesn't fall down as you carry him. Place it in front of where you will be sitting. Then return to the shelf for the second circle with the table on it.

Bring the second green circle to the storytelling circle. Then return to the shelves and bring the basket with the people of the world and the small container.

Put the two green circles next to each other, touching. The one on the right in front of you, the storyteller, is the Good Shepherd, and the one on your left is the table. Put the basket to your right and a little behind where you are sitting. The point is to get this out of the way, so it will not distract the children until you are ready to use it.

The sheepfold, sheep, and shepherd are arranged as shown here.

Words

Watch carefully where I go so you will know where to find this material. Watch with your eyes.

You see, there is a lot to bring. This is big work. Watch carefully.

The Shepherd and the Sheepfold (Storyteller's Perspective)

Movements

Sit for a brief time to let the children settle. If they have trouble getting ready, work with them until they are settled. Then begin.

Touch the head of the Good Shepherd figure.

Run your thumb down the back of the neck of each sheep.

Words

There was once someone who did such wonderful things and said such amazing things that people wondered who he was. Finally they just couldn't help it. They had to ask him who he was.

When they asked him who he was, he said, "I am the Good Shepherd."

"I know each one of my sheep by name, and they know the sound of my voice."

"When I take the sheep from the sheepfold, they follow me."

Movements	Words

Movements

Move the Good Shepherd out of the sheep-fold and around to your right. Move him smoothly (do not hop him along). Move him halfway around to the position at the bottom of the circle in front of you. Then go back and move each one of the sheep to catch up with him. Move them smoothly (do not hop them along). They stay in a single file. Keep silence while you are doing this and just enjoy watching the sheep.

Outside the Sheepfold (Storyteller's Perspective)

"I walk in front of the sheep to show them the way."

Move the Good Shepherd from the bottom position on the right circle to the top position on the left circle. Take your time.

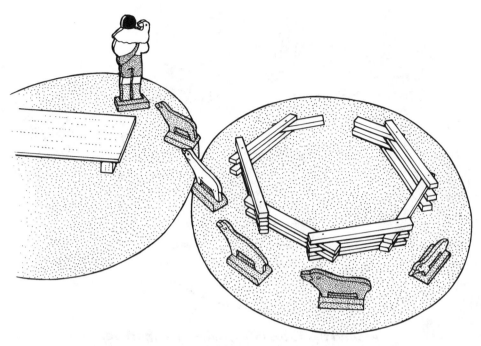

Approaching the Table (Storyteller's Perspective)

Movements

Move the sheep up to where the Good Shepherd is. Move them one at a time. Think about what is happening as you move them from one circle to the other.

Without saying anything else, move the Good Shepherd to the bottom position of the left-hand circle (from the storyteller's perspective) ready to turn and face the table. Move the sheep so that they are spread out evenly around the table but still turned as if they are following around the edge of the circle.

When all of the sheep are in position, move the Good Shepherd forward to stand behind the table (from the children's perspective).

Turn all of the sheep so they are facing the table.

Words

"I show them the way to the good grass."

Around the Table (Storyteller's Perspective)

Movements	**Words**
	This is the table of the Good Shepherd.
Trace the rim of the table.	
Get the chalice and paten from the basket and place them on the table.	
	Here is the bread and wine of the Good Shepherd. Sometimes it seems like we need to have something on the table to remind us that this is the table of the Good Shepherd, but the Good Shepherd is in the bread and the wine, so we don't really need anything to remind us.
	Sometimes someone comes to read the very words of the Good Shepherd, and to give us the bread and the wine.
Remove the Good Shepherd. Bring out the priest or minister and move the priest or minister into the position behind the table where the Good Shepherd was.	

Movements

Take one of the adult human figures from the basket. Hold the figure in the palm of your hand as you show it around the circle to the children, then put it between the sheep. Continue doing this until all the adults from around the world are in place.

Take out the child figures and put them by the adult figures. Do not group the figures by gender, ethnicity, or culture. The world no longer works like that.

Words

Sometimes the people of the world come to this table, and . . .

. . . of course the children come.

The People Around the Table (Storyteller's Perspective)

Movements

Sit and look at the people of the world around the table for a moment, then begin the wondering.

Trace the outline of the table with your finger. Don't hurry the children. Give them time to wonder.

Move your hand over both circles.

When the wondering draws to a close return the materials back to their place on the shelves. Then turn the children's attention toward getting out their work.

Words

Now I wonder if you have ever come close to a table like this?

I wonder where this table could really be?

I wonder if the people are happy around this table?

I wonder if you have ever heard the words of the Good Shepherd?

I wonder if you have ever come close to the bread and the wine?

I wonder where the bread and the wine could really be?

I wonder what the bread and wine could really be?

I wonder where this whole place could really be?

I wonder what your work will be today? You might make something about this story, or another story that you know. Maybe you want to work on something else. There are so many things you can choose from. Only you know what is right for you.

Lesson 13

The Synagogue and the Upper Room[3]

The Holy Word and the Holy Table

How to Use This Lesson

- Core Presentation
- Liturgical Action Lesson: Lessons about sacraments or traditions of the church, which primarily use ritual and symbol to make meaning.
- As the thirteenth lesson in Volume 4 of *The Complete Guide to Godly Play*, it can be presented at any time, but is often presented after Easter.
- It is part of a comprehensive approach to Christian formation that consists of eight volumes. Together the lessons form a spiral curriculum that enables children to move into adolescence with an inner working knowledge of the classical Christian language system to sustain them all their lives.

The Material

- Location: Lent/Easter Shelf Unit
- Pieces: Model of a synagogue, scroll, clay jar, lectern, figure of Jesus, model of the Upper Room, table
- Underlay: None

Background

The first part of the presentation evokes the Liturgy of the Word, which the Christian church developed from the readings of the Jewish synagogue. The second part of the presentation evokes the Liturgy of the Table, which Jesus instituted during the Last Supper in the Upper Room. The Synagogue and Upper Room are joined together to form a model of Christian worship, the joining of the Old and New Testaments, and much more.

---

3 This lesson was suggested by the work of Sofia Cavelletti. The reader should be aware, however, that both the teaching material and the lesson are substantially changed and put to a different use in Godly Play than in her work. Please see Jerome Berryman's *The Spiritual Guidance of Children* (2013), which explores the relationship between Montessori and Cavelletti in Chapters 2 and 3, for further information.

The event in the synagogue is based mainly on Luke 4:16–30, but there are overtones of Mark 6:1–6 and Matthew 13:53–58. Luke tells the larger story, but Matthew and Mark have the famous saying about a prophet being without honor in his own country and in his own house.

Notes on the Material

Find this material on the top shelf of the Lent/Easter Shelf Unit, to the right of the material for the Faces of Easter (*Volume 4*, Lessons 2–8). The material has two main parts, a model of a synagogue and a model of the Upper Room. They are kept separate on the shelf.

The synagogue model includes a clay jar with a scroll in it and a lectern from which the scroll is read. On a scroll is written the text of Luke 4:18–19, quoting Isaiah 61:1–2a. The back wall of the synagogue is made up of three pieces that can be removed. The outer piece of the back wall has a menorah on one side and a cross on the other. The two inner pieces of the back wall will form two walls of the finished building made by joining the synagogue to the Upper Room.

The menorah is a seven-lamp lampstand that has been a symbol of Judaism since ancient times. It was revealed by Moses to be used in the Tabernacle (Exodus 25:31–40). The lamps burn pure olive oil. Candles were not known in the Middle East until about 400 CE.

The model of the Upper Room has a table in it. There is also a cast metal figure of Jesus, used in both the synagogue and the Upper Room. On the shelf, this figure can be left standing in the Upper Room. There are no figures for the synagogue congregation or for the Twelve, because in this presentation the focus is entirely on Jesus.

Special Notes

When telling this story, be careful with your movements, especially when lifting the two back pieces from the synagogue wall. It's easy to knock them down with a loud clatter and disrupt the mood of the lesson. We also recommend picking up the Jesus figure separately from the rest of the material because he falls over easily.

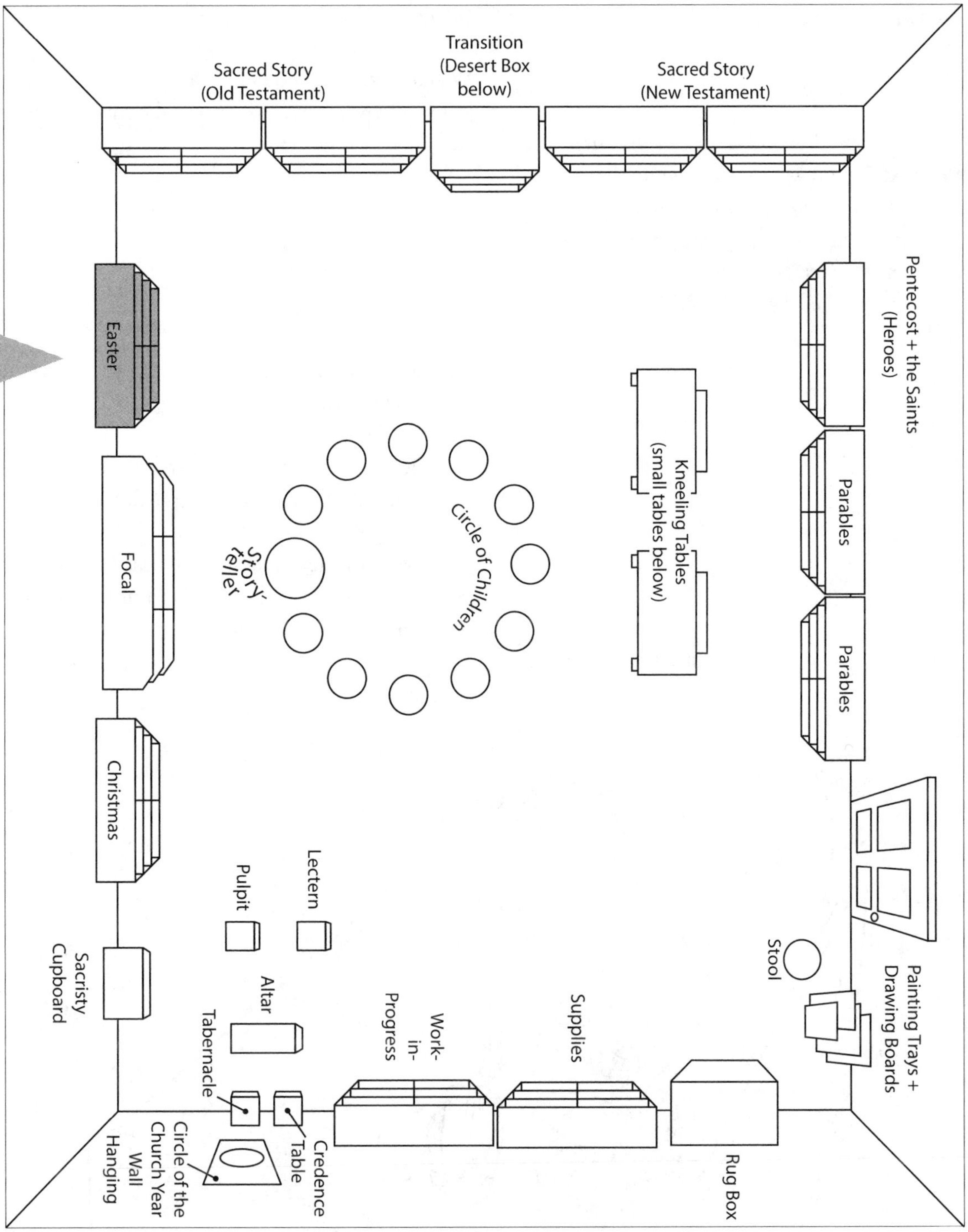
Sacred Story
(Old Testament)
Transition
(Desert Box
below)
Sacred Story
(New Testament)
Pentecost + the Saints
(Heroes)
Easter
Parables
Parables
Kneeling Tables
(small tables below)
Circle of Children
Story-teller
Focal
Christmas
Lectern
Pulpit
Stool
Painting Trays +
Drawing Boards
Sacristy
Cupboard
Altar
Work-
in-
Progress
Supplies
Tabernacle
Credence
Table
Circle of the
Church Year
Wall
Hanging
Rug Box

Where to Find Materials

Movements

When the children are settled in the circle, get the model of the synagogue, the model of the Upper Room, and the figure of Jesus. Move the synagogue into the circle of children. The cross on the back wall is hidden, facing you. The menorah on the back wall is toward the children.

Place the Jesus figure in the model synagogue.

Words

Watch where I go to get today's story so you will know where to find it if you make this your work.

This is the synagogue in the village of Nazareth, where Jesus grew up.

After Jesus came back from the desert across the River Jordan, he came home to Nazareth.

Jesus went to the synagogue, as was his custom. He went to the reading place and unrolled the scroll of Isaiah.

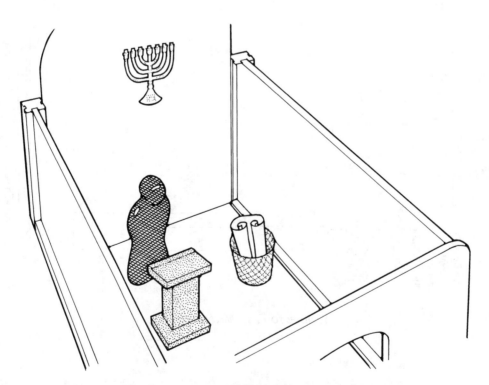

The Synagogue (Children's Perspective)

Movements	**Words**
	This is what he read:
Unroll the scroll that is in the jar and read from it. This is Luke 4:18–19 quoting Isaiah 61:1–2a.	"The Spirit of the Lord is upon me, because he has anointed me to preach good news to the poor. He has sent me to proclaim release to the captives and recovery of sight to the blind, to let the oppressed go free, to proclaim the year of the Lord's favor."
	Jesus rolled up the scroll and sat down.
Roll up the scroll and place it back in the jar.	When they began to discuss the reading, he said something like, "Today this scripture has been fulfilled in your hearing. It has come true."
	The people heard what Jesus said and became angry. He is not the Messiah! They knew who he was. He was Mary and Joseph's son.
	They took Jesus to the edge of the village where there was a cliff. They wanted to throw him off . . .
Move the Jesus figure out from the synagogue to stand in front of it.	
	. . . but he walked back through the crowd and into the hills.
Remove the Jesus figure and place it beside you.	
	Many months went by. He gathered the Twelve. He did his work. Then he turned to Jerusalem for the last time. Jesus and the Twelve came into the city on a Sunday. He taught in the Temple on Monday, Tuesday, and Wednesday. On Thursday, the Temple guards could not find him.
	That evening Jesus and the Twelve went through the dark and narrow streets. They climbed upstairs in a house. They went into the Upper Room and shared their last supper together.
Move the Upper Room model into the middle of the circle of children and place it beside the synagogue model. Put the Jesus figure behind the table in the middle.	

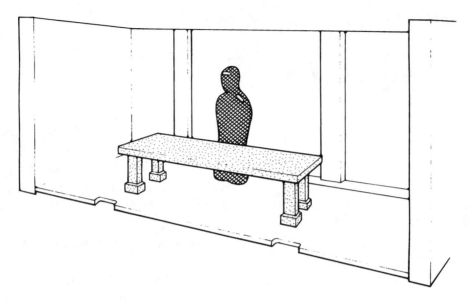

The Upper Room (Children's Perspective)

Movements

Words

After they had eaten everything they wanted to eat, Jesus did something very strange. He took a piece of bread, gave thanks to God for it, broke it, and shared it with the Twelve.

Then he said something like, "When you share the bread like this, I will be there."

But he was there!

Then he took a cup of wine, gave thanks to God for it, and shared it with them.

Then he said something like, "When you share the wine like this, I will be there."

He was always saying things like that. What could he mean? They did not understand at first, but they did not forget. Later they would understand.

Now watch carefully.

Movements

Move the synagogue model around in front of the Upper Room, with its back wall touching the front edge of the Upper Room. Slide the outer piece of the back wall of the synagogue off and place it to the side.

Take the two remaining panels that make up the inner back wall of the synagogue and slide one into each of the slots formed by the inner front edges of the Upper Room and the outer back edges of the synagogue. This makes two models into one model of a cross-shaped church. Lastly, slide the outer piece of the back wall onto the newly formed church with the cross facing the children.

Words

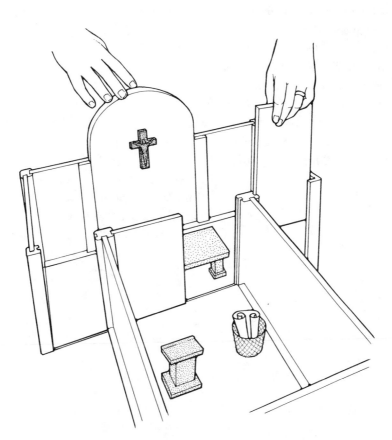

**Changing the Synagogue and the Upper Room
into the Church (Children's Perspective)**

Movements

Words

Look. I wonder what this could be?

Hmm.

Trace the structure with your finger.

Point to the reading lectern. Point to the table. Trace the area of the synagogue and the Upper Room and then trace the whole structure again. Do not say anything. Let the children make the discoveries.

If they do not say anything aloud, continue to wonder silently and then begin to put the material away.

Now watch carefully where I go to put this away, so you will always know where to find it.

Separate the model of the synagogue from the Upper Room. Take your time as you are modeling how to do this for the children. Be sure you put the back wall of the synagogue in place with the menorah showing. Then return everything to the shelf.

Return to the circle, then turn the children's attention toward getting out their own work.

I wonder what your work will be today? You might make something about this story, or another story that you know. Maybe you want to work on something else. There are so many things you can choose from. Only you know what is right for you.

Lesson 14

The Circle of the Holy Eucharist

What happens when we share the bread and wine in church?

How to Use This Lesson

- Core Presentation
- Liturgical Action Lesson: Lessons about sacraments or traditions of the church, which primarily use ritual and symbol to make meaning.
- As the fourteenth lesson in Volume 4 of *The Complete Guide to Godly Play*, it can be presented any Sunday in the church year.
- It is part of a comprehensive approach to Christian formation that consists of eight volumes. Together the lessons form a spiral curriculum that enables children to move into adolescence with an inner working knowledge of the classical Christian language system to sustain them all their lives.

The Material

- Location: Lent/Easter Shelf Unit
- Pieces: Wooden tray, one wooden plaque picturing Jesus in the Upper Room, one wooden plaque picturing Jesus in the synagogue, set of seventeen wooden plaques showing the major parts and acts of the Holy Eucharist
- Underlay: Green felt circle (approximately thirty-six inches or ninety-one centimeters in diameter)

Background

This presentation and material, another in the series of lessons developing themes in the Holy Eucharist, helps children pull together the sequence of liturgical actions and images from the Godly Play presentations they have seen and from their church's Sunday celebration. Adjust it, as necessary, to fit what happens in your church or denomination.

We lay out the lesson on a green circle, echoing the green used in the presentation of the Good Shepherd and World Communion. Its circular shape is important, because when the Holy Eucharist concludes, it is ready to begin again, waiting for us to take part. The gift of its way to make meaning is always there, inviting us to begin again.

The pieces laid out on the green circle are flat, two-dimensional pieces rather than the three-dimensional pieces the children have seen so far in this series. This lesson helps children take a step toward abstraction and the integration of the parts into the wholeness of the Eucharist.

Notes on the Material

Find this material on the far right of the middle shelf of the Lent/Easter Shelf Unit, directly underneath the material for Synagogue and the Upper Room. The material is a wooden tray holding a green circular felt underlay and a set of wooden plaques.

As the lesson begins, the presentation retells the story of the Synagogue and the Upper Room, but this time, instead of using three-dimensional materials, you put an orange-trimmed plaque in the center of the green circle showing a drawing of Jesus reading in the synagogue and then below it a yellow-trimmed plaque with a drawing of Jesus and the Twelve in the Upper Room. These two plaques measure four inches by six and one-half inches (ten by seventeen centimeters).

You then lay out plaques around the edge of the circle to show the major acts in the sequence of the Holy Eucharist. If necessary, make adjustments to the plaques to match the practice of your congregation. You may need to find someone to draw you different images, or you could take photographs of what happens at the key moments in your church's celebration of communion to create your own material. Change any words of the lesson, too, to match what is actually said and done in your church.

The key plaque bears the words "The Holy Eucharist." This is an orange-trimmed plaque that measures five inches by seven and one-half inches (thirteen by nineteen centimeters). The center of the plaque shows the picture of a golden cross. Two additional plaques, each measuring four inches by six and one-half inches (ten by seventeen centimeters), mark the two major divisions of the Holy Eucharist: "The Word of God" and "The Holy Communion." The Word of God plaque is orange-trimmed with a drawing of an open Bible. The Holy Communion plaque is yellow-trimmed with a drawing of a host and chalice to represent the bread and wine.

We suggest eight orange-trimmed plaques, each four inches by six and one-half inches (ten by seventeen centimeters), with the following labels for the Liturgy of the Word:

- Opening and the Collect of the Day
- The Lessons: The Old Testament—The Letters
- Lesson: the Gospel
- The Sermon
- The Nicene Creed
- The Prayers of the People
- Confession of Sin
- The Peace

We suggest six yellow-trimmed plaques, each four inches by six and one-half inches (ten by seventeen centimeters), with the following labels for the Liturgy of Holy Communion:

- Offertory
- The Great Thanksgiving
- Prayer of Consecration
- The Breaking of the Bread
- Communion
- Blessing and Dismissal

Special Notes

Please note that extra sets of these cards make a wonderful way for children to follow and name what is going on in the liturgy of your church. You can purchase laminated sets from Godly Play Resources. They come on notebook rings so the children can follow the action by flipping the cards. Of course if you are using different plaques because your church's practice is different, you will need to make your own.

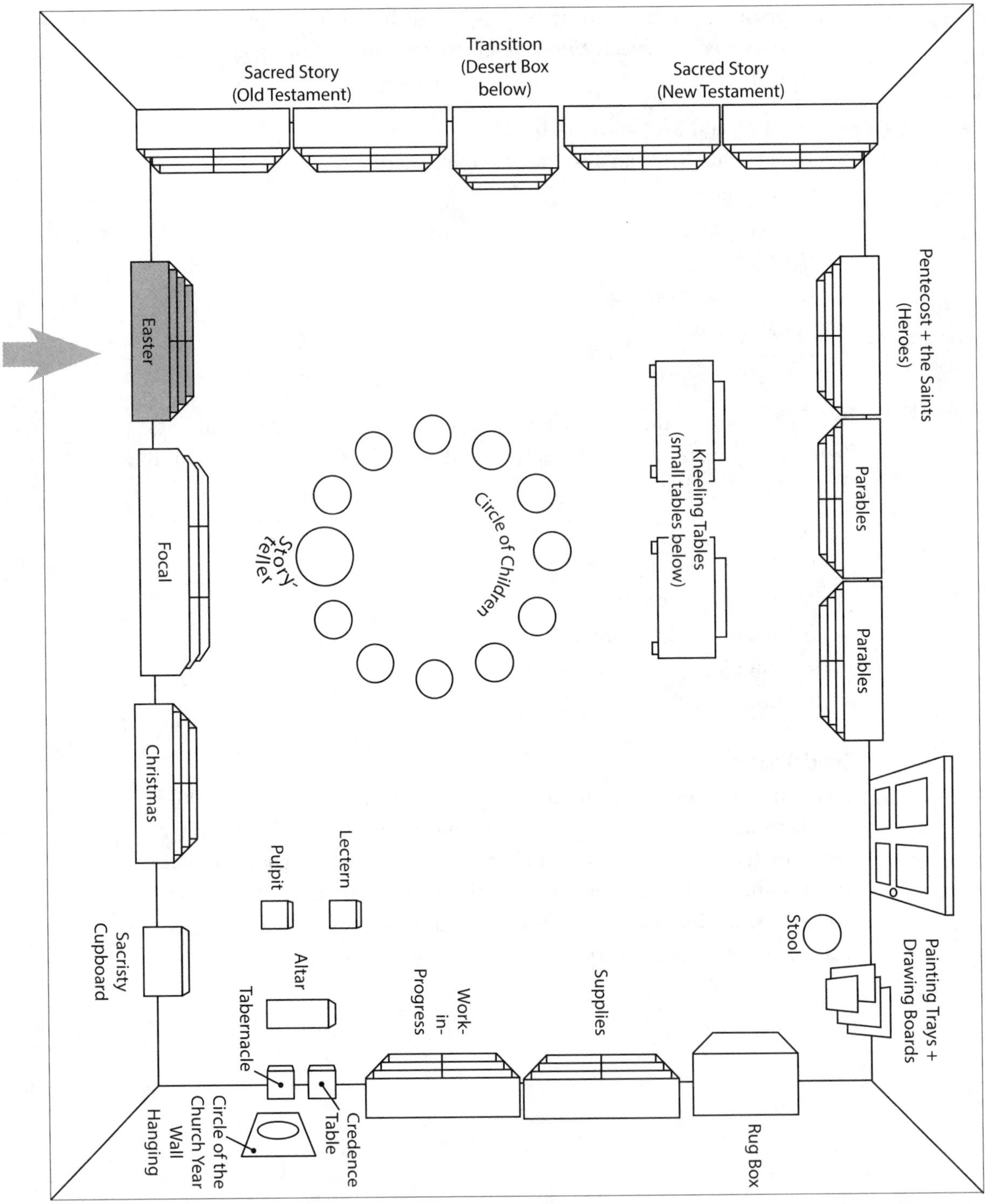

Sacred Story
(Old Testament)
Transition
(Desert Box
below)
Sacred Story
(New Testament)
Pentecost + the Saints
(Heroes)
Easter
Kneeling Tables
(small tables below)
Parables
Parables
Focal
Story-
teller
Circle of Children
Christmas
Lectern
Pulpit
Painting Trays +
Drawing Boards
Stool
Sacristy
Cupboard
Altar
Work-
in-
Progress
Supplies
Tabernacle
Credence
Table
Circle of the
Church Year
Wall
Hanging
Rug Box

Where to Find Materials

Movements

When the children are settled in the circle, go to the Lent/Easter Shelf Unit and bring the tray with its underlay and plaques to the circle.

Take out the underlay as if it were the underlay for a Parable. Leave it crumpled in the middle of the circle for a moment, and then smooth it out. It is the same color as the underlay for the Parable of the Good Shepherd.

The children may or may not respond, helping to build a metaphor and connecting it to previous lessons. If they do respond, wonder with them for a few moments, but this does not need to go on as long as with a Parable.

Then begin the lesson.

Place the plaque for the synagogue in the center of the underlay, facing the children.

Words

Watch where I go, so you will always know where to find this lesson.

I wonder what this could be.

After Jesus was baptized and had come back over the River Jordan from the desert, he went home to his village of Nazareth.

He went into the synagogue and read from the scroll of Isaiah:

"The Spirit of the Lord is upon me, because he has anointed me to preach good news to the poor. He has sent me to proclaim release to the captives and recovery of sight to the blind, to let the oppressed go free, to proclaim the year of the Lord's favor." (Luke 4:18–19)

Jesus rolled up the scroll, handed it to an attendant and sat down. He then said to the people, "Today this scripture has been fulfilled in your hearing."

Movements	Words
	The people of Jesus' village said something like: "This is not the Messiah, the Anointed One. He thinks he is God, but he is just Mary and Joseph's son."
	They took Jesus to the edge of the village where there was a cliff. They wanted to throw him off, but he walked back through the crowd and into the hills.
	Many months went by. He gathered the Twelve. He did his work. Then he turned to Jerusalem for the last time.
Place the plaque with Jesus and the Twelve in the center of the underlay, below the synagogue card, facing the children.	
	On Thursday of that last week, Jesus and the Twelve met in an Upper Room. After they had everything they wanted to eat and drink, Jesus did something very strange. He took a piece of bread, and when he had given thanks, he broke it, and shared it with the Twelve. Then he said something like, "When you share the bread like this I will be there."
	They must have thought, "What do you mean? You are here."
	He then took a cup of wine. He gave thanks to God for it and said something like, "Whenever you share the cup of wine like this, I will be there." The Twelve did not understand, but they never forgot. Later they would understand.
	This was how the Holy Eucharist began.
Place the Holy Eucharist plaque facing the children (12:00 position from the children's perspective).	
	It has two parts.

Movements

Point to the orange plaque of the synagogue already placed at the center of the underlay.

Place the plaque for "The Word of God" just to your left of the Holy Eucharist plaque.

Point to the yellow plaque of the Upper Room already placed the center of the underlay.

Place the plaque for "The Holy Communion" near the children's bottom of the circle, the point farthest from you. Place it a little to your right of the midpoint of the circle (between 6:00 and 7:00 from the children's perspective).

You will now place plaques in a clockwise fashion between the plaque for "The Word of God" and the plaque for "The Holy Communion." First place the plaque for the "Opening and Collect of the Day." The word "collect" has an emphasis on the first syllable (kaw-lect).

Place the plaque for "The Lessons: The Old Testament—The Letters."

Place the plaque for "The Lessons: The Gospel."

Words

First there is the Liturgy of the Word of God.

The Word of God is when we read from the scriptures and hear the sermon.

The second part is the Holy Communion.

When the Holy Eucharist begins, there is sometimes music and a procession but there does not need to be. The priest says, "Blessed be God: Father, Son, and Holy Spirit." Prayers are said to help us get ready. One of the prayers changes each week. It is called a "collect."

Someone then comes forward and reads from the Old Testament. Next we often read or sing a psalm. Then someone reads something from the New Testament, perhaps part of one of Paul's letters.

Movements	Words
	After that the most important reading happens. It is the Gospel. The Gospel Book is carried very carefully to the center, and sometimes there are even people on each side of the reader holding tall candles called "torches." Everyone stands to hear the Gospel.
Place the plaque for "The Sermon."	After the reading of God's Word in the Bible, someone comes and tries to say something about what was read. This is called "the Sermon." It is not easy. Sometimes you have to listen very carefully. This is hard for the grownups, too.
Place the plaque for "The Nicene Creed."	After the sermon we all say together what we believe. One person got to say something in the sermon. Now we all speak. Together we say the Nicene Creed.
Place the plaque for "The Prayers of the People."	Next we pray for everyone. We pray for people who are sick or in trouble. We pray for those who are hungry or lost. We pray for peace. We also give thanks for all the wonderful things that happen in life—like babies being born, people getting married, and sick people getting well. We give thanks for good governments and for the lives of people who have died.
Place the plaque for "The Confession of Sin."	The leader then says, "Let us confess our sins against God and our neighbor." No one is perfect, so we all ask for forgiveness.
	Sometimes even when good people try hard, they still make mistakes. We need to say we are sorry to people we have hurt and to God. It is good to confess our sins. It helps us to do better next time.
	After we confess our sins all together, the priest tells us that *God* forgives us and strengthens us in all goodness.

Movements	Words
Place the plaque for "The Peace" at the children's bottom of the circle (6:00 from the children's perspective). This brings the plaques for the Word of God to an end.	
	After we are forgiven, we can't help but want to be close to everyone, so people turn to each other and say, "The peace of the Lord be always with you." People say back, "And also with you."
Now you have come to the plaque for "The Holy Communion." The next set of plaques will also be placed in clockwise fashion, from the plaque for "The Holy Communion" to the plaque for "The Holy Eucharist."	
	Look, now we change. The time of the readings and thinking about them is over. The prayers have been said. We now get ready to do something very different. We prepare for Holy Communion. It helps us go where words and thinking alone cannot take us.
Place the plaque for "The Offertory."	People bring gifts of money and other things to the altar. Above all they bring the gifts of bread and wine. The gifts are received and placed on the altar.
Place the plaque for "The Great Thanksgiving."	When everything is ready the priest begins the Great Thanksgiving: "The Lord be with you." This is a time to lift up our hearts, to give thanks and praise. What is beginning to happen is a great mystery.
	We remember the Last Supper of Jesus and the Twelve . . .
Point to the plaque with the picture of Jesus and the Twelve at the Last Supper and then to the plaque for "The Great Thanksgiving."	
Place the plaque for the "Prayer of Consecration."	. . . and then gradually we are there and it is here.

Movements	Words
	The priest prays for the Holy Spirit to sanctify the bread and wine, to change them from their ordinary use to this special use. The priest also prays for us to be sanctified, so we will be able to faithfully receive this holy Sacrament and serve God in unity, constancy, and peace, and at the last day to join with all the saints in the joy of God's eternal kingdom.
	We then say together the Lord's Prayer and hear especially the part: "Give us this day our daily bread."
Place the plaque for "The Breaking of Bread."	The priest holds the bread up so we can see it, and breaks it. Sometimes you can even hear it break. We give thanks for Jesus being with us and the priest reminds us that the bread and wine are for us, gifts from God.
Place the plaque for "Communion."	People come forward now to receive the holy bread and holy wine. Jesus is with us in the bread and wine and we are all together, all over the world, and with all who have lived and died in this huge family of families called "the Church."
Place the plaque for the "Blessing and Dismissal."	Everything is put away and we get ready to go out. The leader says something like, "Let us go forth in the name of Christ."
	And we always say, all together, "Thanks be to God."
	The Holy Eucharist is ready to begin again.
The green underlay now has plaques all around its circumference. Sit back and enjoy the completed presentation for a moment or two. Then begin the wondering.	

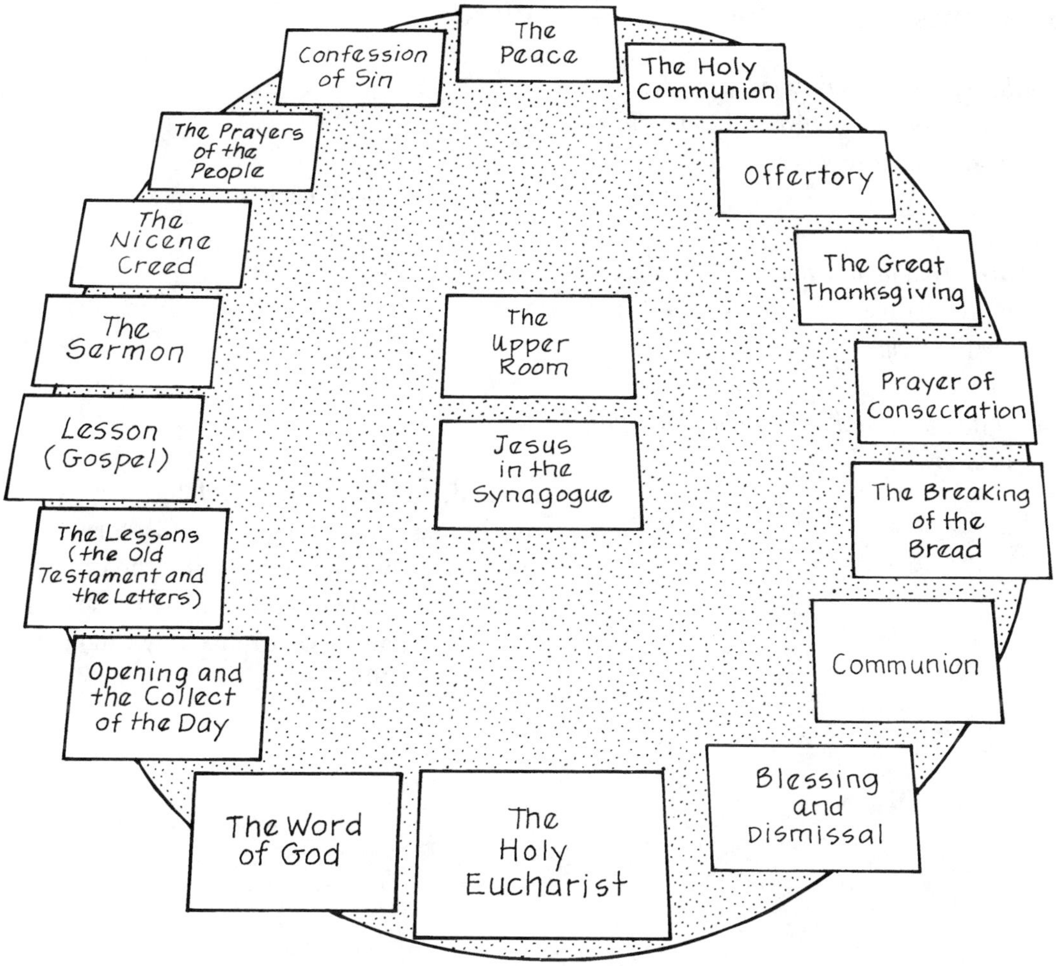

The Completed Circle (Children's Perspective)

Movements

Move your hand around the circumference.

Words

I wonder what part of the Holy Eucharist you like best?

I wonder what part is the most important part?

I wonder what part is especially for you?

I wonder if we could leave anything out and still have everything we need?

Movements

When the wondering is finished, carefully replace the plaques in the tray. As you replace the plaques, name them once again.

Don't hurry. Fold up the underlay and place it in the tray. Carry the tray with two hands and place it on the shelf.

Return to the circle and begin to help the children choose their work.

Words

Here is the Holy Eucharist. Here is the part called "the Word of God" . . .

I wonder what your work will be today? You might make something about this story, or another story that you know. Maybe you want to work on something else. There are so many things you can choose from. Only you know what is right for you.

Lesson 15

Symbols of the Holy Eucharist

Special Materials for the Holy Eucharist

How to Use This Lesson

- Extension Presentation
- Liturgical Action Lesson: Lessons about sacraments or traditions of the church, which primarily use ritual and symbol to make meaning.
- As the fifteenth lesson in Volume 4 of *The Complete Guide to Godly Play*, it can be presented any Sunday in the church year, but preferably early in the year so that the children know how to use it appropriately.
- "Extensions" extend the Core Lessons. They extend not only Sacred Stories but also the Liturgical and Parable lessons. Extension Lessons sit on the shelves below these lessons, since Core Lessons are displayed on the top shelf in the Godly Play room. This lesson extends the Circle of the Holy Eucharist (*Volume 4,* Lesson 14).
- It is part of a comprehensive approach to Christian formation that consists of eight volumes. Together the lessons form a spiral curriculum that enables children to move into adolescence with an inner working knowledge of the classical Christian language system to sustain them all their lives.

The Material

- Location: Area of the room set apart for these symbols
- Pieces: Wooden liturgical furnishings (tabernacle, credence table, lectern, altar, pulpit, sacristy cupboard); cloth furnishings (seasonal hangings, fair linen, purificators); other furnishings (Bible, candles, candle sticks, candle snuffer, altar book, Gospel Book, cruets for water and wine, ciborium, chalice, paten); box of prompting cards (wooden plaques containing the name of each item)
- Underlay: None

Background

This presentation requires an elaborate set of materials described below. The reading portions of the presentation are intended for children from about the second grade on.

This lesson supports children by introducing and naming the actual symbols, so they can work independently with the Godly Play material. In the Godly Play room, they can use all their senses instead of primarily relying on sight. This gives them more experience to draw on when they see actual symbols, such as the chalice and paten, etc., in church.

The fundamental goal of this lesson is to convey that these things are set apart from ordinary use for special use in the Holy Eucharist. To show this, we give almost everything another name. For example, a cup is no longer a cup. It becomes a chalice. This new language sharpens all the children's senses to participate in the liturgical action when the congregation gathers, both in the church and elsewhere.

If your tradition uses different items from the ones listed below, we encourage you to adapt the lesson to more closely resemble your use.

This lesson is categorized as an extension material, because it extends (adds details) to the Circle of the Holy Eucharist. These lessons are generally reserved for more experienced children, but this one is an exception as the material is both attractive and suitable for young children. We advise that it be introduced early in the year so that the children can use it appropriately.

Notes on the Material

This material is kept in an area of the room all its own. Instead of bringing the material to a group of children, you bring a small group (not more than three children) to the materials and work with them there.

The setup includes:

- a small wooden tabernacle (box), attached to the wall
- a credence table (small shelf), attached to the wall
- a sacristy cupboard
- an altar (table)
- a pulpit
- a lectern

The diagram on page 146 shows the layout of the above items.

There is also a box that holds "prompting cards" for naming the symbols of the Holy Eucharist. The wooden materials, cards, seasonal cloth hangings, a fair linen, and purificators are made by Godly Play Resources.

Other materials you may wish to include are child-sized communion materials, such as could be found in a portable communion kit. (Contact your sacristan or a church supplies distributor that ministers to your denomination.) You will want to include the liturgical materials for your denomination, such as *The Book of Common Prayer* (Episcopal), *The Lutheran Book of Worship*, and so on.

Special Notes

When you introduce this material to young children, gather them in front of the material in a half-circle facing the altar. After setting up the materials, the storyteller sits inside, between the tabernacle and the altar to present the lesson. A child working alone sits where the storyteller does. When children are working in a group they take turns being the one child who sits where the storyteller does.

Sometimes children will spontaneously set the table and act out what they see in church. This is "playing church" in the best sense. The play is not silly or trivial. It is about the symbols, how they are used, and order of the ritual. On a deeper level they are expressing with their bodies what they have absorbed both in this lesson and in their experiences in church. The ultimate goal is for the older children to follow the prayer book and use the symbols and gestures appropriately for the Holy Eucharist.

After presenting this lesson, it is good opportunity to arrange a time for the children to visit the sacristy, meet the people who care for the symbols, and see where everything is kept.

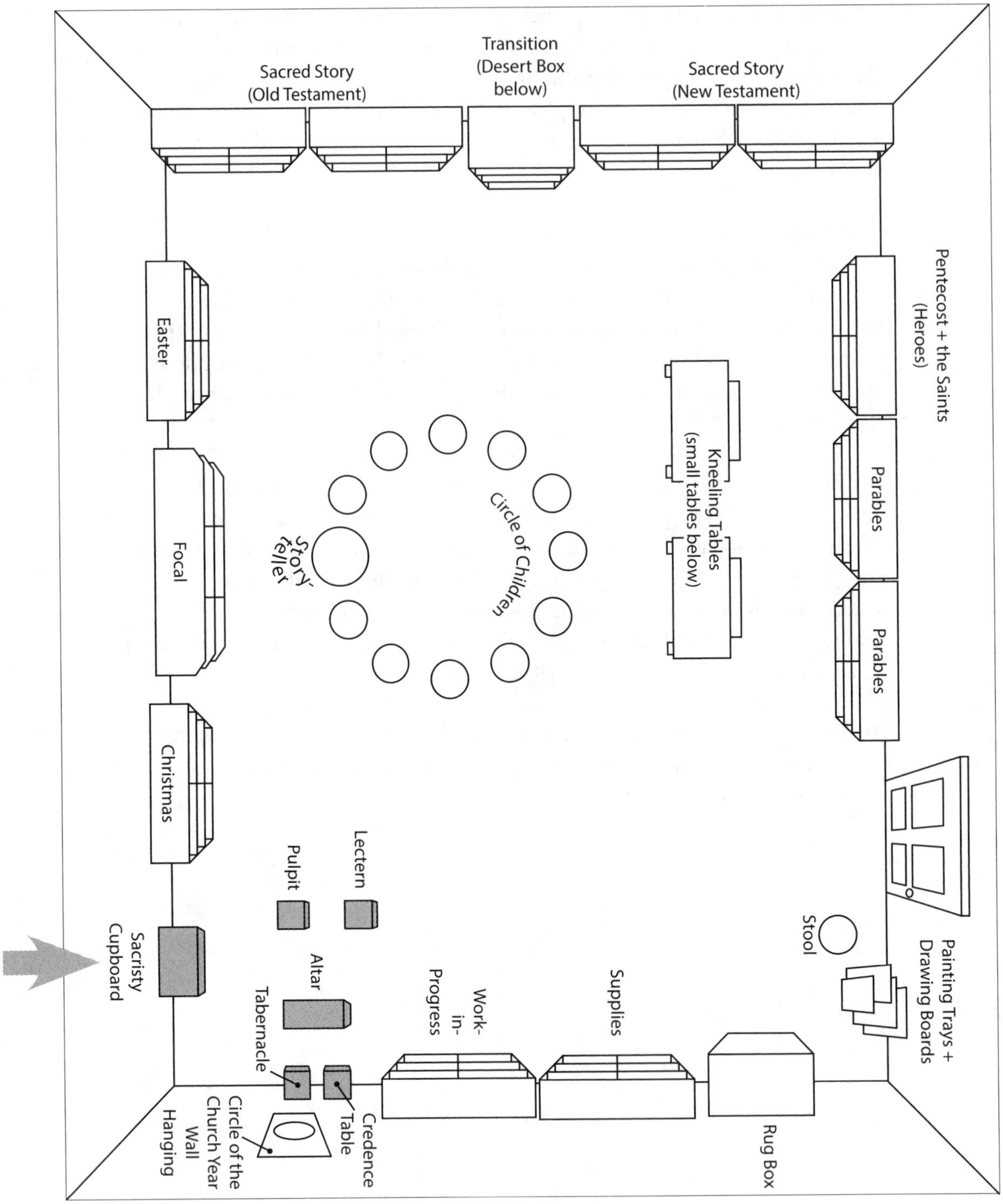
Transition
(Desert Box
below)
Sacred Story
(Old Testament)
Sacred Story
(New Testament)
Easter
Focal
Christmas
Sacristy
Cupboard
Pentecost + the Saints
(Heroes)
Parables
Parables
Kneeling Tables
(small tables below)
Circle of Children
Story-
teller
Lectern
Pulpit
Altar
Tabernacle
Credence
Table
Circle of the
Church Year
Wall
Hanging
Work-
in-
Progress
Supplies
Rug Box
Stool
Painting Trays +
Drawing Boards

Where to Find Materials

Movements

Bring the children with whom you are working to the area where the symbols are kept. The storyteller stands or kneels beside the material so that it is easy to gather all that is needed and names all of the furniture using the prompting cards.

Show the children the prompting card that says "sacristy" and place it on the cabinet.

Show the children the prompting card that says "altar" and place it on the altar.

Show the children the prompting card that says "lectern" and place it on the lectern.

Point to the Bible.

Show the children the prompting card that says "pulpit" and place it on the pulpit.

Show the children the prompting card that says "tabernacle" and place it on the tabernacle. If children ask about this you can explain that this is where we put the left over bread and wine. It can be brought to people who cannot come to church.

Open the drawers of the cabinet and remove the hangings and other cloth furnishings used in the celebration of Holy Communion.

Words

Here is the sacristy cabinet. Inside are many things that we will name soon. Here are the drawers. They contain more of the things we will need for this lesson.

This is the altar, like where Holy Communion takes place in church. Here is the stand for the altar book and here is the book.

This is the lectern, like where the lessons are read in church.

Here is the Bible that the lessons come from.

This is the pulpit, like where the sermon is preached in church.

This is the tabernacle, like where the holy bread and holy wine are kept, in church.

Let's see what is inside the drawers of the sacristy cabinet first.

Movements

Move the prompting card that says "altar" to the side, leaning it up against one of the legs, facing the children. Move the altar book stand and prayer book to the floor so that you can prepare the altar.

Put the appropriate colored altar hanging on the altar. Model for the children how to do this.

Put these hangings in place.

Spread the fair linen on the altar, smoothing it out carefully. Find the prompting card that says "fair linen" and place it on the altar. Now you can also return the altar book stand and prayer book to the altar (on the left or right side, leaving room to set up the chalice and paten).

Lay the purificator on the altar.

Find the prompting card that says "purificator" and place it beside the purificator.

Open the doors of the sacristy cabinet to find the other symbols needed for the lesson.

Take out the cruets and place them on the altar. Find the prompting card that says "cruet" and place it beside them.

Words

Here are altar coverings. Look. There is one for every time or season in the church year—green for the "green and growing times," purple for Advent and Lent, white for Christmas and Easter, red for Pentecost.

You can always see what color to use by looking at the "Circle of the Church Year." What color should we use today?

There are also colors for the lectern and the pulpit.

Here is the fair linen.

Here is the purificator.

It looks like a napkin, but we call it a purificator.

Now we will open these doors and take out the most important things.

Here are the cruets—one for the water and one for the wine.

Movements

Take out the paten and lay it on the altar.

Find the prompting card that says "paten" and place it beside the paten.

Take out the chalice and lay it on the altar.

Find the prompting card that says "chalice" and place it beside the chalice.

Quietly observe all of the things that you have prepared.

For any symbol or symbols you choose to introduce in this presentation, use a three-step procedure in which you identify, value, and name the symbol. This is the classic Montessori three-period lesson. For example, for the chalice, follow these three steps.

1. Point to the chalice or hold it up.

2. Put the chalice down with the other symbols and let the children point out the chalice.

3. Point to the chalice.

With older children, you can elaborate this third step.

Repeat this process with each of the symbols. You can stop at any point if the circle of children begins to lose energy. You can always return to the material at another time and introduce more of the symbols.

Words

This is the paten.

It looks like a plate, but we call it a paten. It holds the holy bread in church.

This is the chalice.

It looks like a cup, but we call it a chalice. It holds the holy wine in church.

Now everything is here. Let's see if we can name everything.

This is the chalice.

Show me the chalice.

What is this?

Where is it kept?

What is it used for?

Movements

When you have introduced several symbols, you can begin the wondering.

Words

I wonder which of these things you like best?

I wonder which one you think is the most important?

I wonder *where* you see these things in church?

I wonder *when* you see these things in church?

I wonder what the priest (pastor or minister or whatever language your denomination uses) does with these things?

I wonder who cares for these things in the church?

I wonder where they are kept?

I wonder what these things show us?

When the wondering winds down you can put the material away in reverse order. Name each thing as you put it away.

Leave the altar, pulpit, and lectern hangings as well as the fair linen in place. The next time the season of the church year changes you can invite children to choose as their work changing the colors on these materials. If no one chooses it, the storyteller can change the colors during the work period.

When everything is put away, begin to help the children choose their work.

I wonder what your work will be today? You might make something about this story, or another story that you know.

Maybe you want to work on something else? There are so many things you can choose from. Only you know what is right for you.

The Mystery of Pentecost

The People of God Meet God in a New Way
(Genesis 11:1–9, Acts 1:5–14, 2:1–12,
Mark 16:19–20, Luke 24:50–53)

How to Use This Lesson

- Extension Presentation
- Liturgical Action Lesson: Lessons about sacraments or traditions of the church, which primarily use ritual and symbol to make meaning.
- As the sixteenth lesson in Volume 4 of *The Complete Guide to Godly Play*, it is presented on or near the Feast of Pentecost.
- "Extensions" extend the Core Lessons. They extend not only Sacred Stories but also the Liturgical and Parable lessons. Extension Lessons sit on the shelves below these lessons, since Core Lessons are displayed on the top shelf in the Godly Play room. This lesson extends Knowing Jesus in a New Way (*Volume 8*, Lessons 7–13).
- It is part of a comprehensive approach to Christian formation that consists of eight volumes. Together the lessons form a spiral curriculum that enables children to move into adolescence with an inner working knowledge of the classical Christian language system to sustain them all their lives.

The Material

- Location: Pentecost Shelf Unit
- Pieces: Red Parable-sized box, twelve brown felt strips, six plain wooden blocks, symbols of the Twelve Apostles
- Underlay: Red felt (approximately thirty-six inches or ninety centimeters square)

Background

Something strange happened on Pentecost that had to do with "tongues" of fire and speaking so that no matter what "tongues" (languages) people spoke, they could understand what the apostles meant. Did their tongues burn in their mouths as they began to communicate in a new way? Was the communication nonverbal? Can God's presence be communicated in words? There are many questions.

The strange event on the Day of Pentecost reminds us of the earlier time when communication was fractured so that what before had been understandable was now babble, a confusion of tongues. That is why this lesson begins with the Tower of Babel, from Genesis 11:1–9. This presentation also draws on stories found in Mark 16:19–20, Luke 24:50–53, and Acts 1:5–14, 2:1–12.

Notes on the Material

Place the box to the right of Knowing Jesus in a New Way (*Volume 8*, Lessons 7–13) on the top shelf of the Pentecost Shelf Unit. The Introduction to the Communion of Saints (*Volume 7*, Lessons 1 and 2) sits to the right of the Mystery of Pentecost. Below these three lessons are the twelve lessons about the saints found in *Volume 7*.

The box is red and the same size and shape as the parable boxes. Inside the box is a red felt underlay that matches the size and shape of the underlay used in the Parable of the Good Shepherd (*Volume 3*, Lesson 9—about thirty-six inches or ninety-one centimeters square). There are also twelve brown felt strips (about one inch by ten inches or two and a half by twenty-five centimeters) that match the strips from the Parable of the Good Shepherd (*Volume 3*, Lesson 9). The box also holds six plain wooden blocks (about three inches by three inches or five by five centimeters) that can be stacked to make a Tower of Babel. Finally, there is a container that holds the symbols of the Twelve.

Special Notes

This lesson resembles a Parable. Like a Parable, it's meant to be symbolic, rather than historical. Stacking the blocks, however, creates a three-dimensional structure, adding concreteness to the story. We balance this concreteness by using symbols instead of figures for the apostles and brown strips instead of a model for the Upper Room where they were staying when the Holy Spirit came upon them. This moves the presentation toward the parabolic rather than the concrete.

Our intent is to leave room for God to enter and play. Making the presentation too realistic blocks the mystery, shuts the door to God's presence, and turns the event into past history instead of present encounter.

It is helpful to tell the story of the Twelve (*Volume 4*, Lesson 11) before you tell this lesson so that the symbols of the Twelve do not distract during the telling of this lesson.

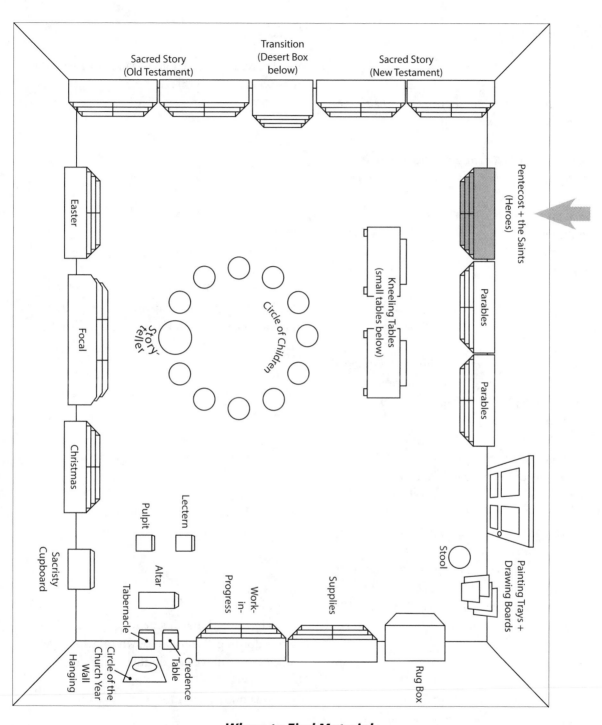

Where to Find Materials

Movements

When the children are settled, go to the shelves where the material is located.

Bring the box to the circle and place it in the center of the children. Sit back. Relax. Be present.

Pick up the red box with mystery and amazement.

Set it back down.

Move the box to your side with the lid propped up on the side facing the children, so they won't be tempted to peek at what is coming out of the box next.

Take out the underlay. Leave it crumpled in the middle of the circle for a moment and then smooth it out. I wonder what this could be?

The children may or may not respond, helping to build a metaphor and connecting it to previous lessons. If they do respond, wonder with them for a few moments, but this does not need to go on as long as with a Parable.

Pause and begin.

Place the first block down in the middle of the underlay.

Put the second block down on top of the first.

Words

Watch carefully where I go so you will always know where to find this material.

I wonder what could be inside?

This looks like a Parable box, but it is red. It must be like a Parable and yet not be a Parable. I have an idea. Let's look inside and see what is there.

There are some things inside to tell the story, but there is nothing else to put down to help us get ready. I guess all we can do then, is begin.

There was once a great tower.

Everyone working on the tower spoke the same language as they worked together.

Movements

Slowly build up the blocks as you tell the story.

Keep building block by block, in such a way that the tower becomes more precarious.

The blocks now need to fall of their own weight.

Slowly pick up the blocks and put them back into the box. Sit back and pause. Reflect silently on what has happened. Then say:

Reach into the box and pull out the brown strips of felt one by one.

Lay out the brown felt strips in a square in the same way you do when telling the Parable of the Good Shepherd, close to you but toward the middle of the underlay.

Make an opening in the same way you do when telling the Parable of the Good Shepherd.

Words

But as the tower grew taller and taller, they began to talk in different ways.

They wanted the tower to reach the heavens.

They grew so proud of themselves that they began to think they were greater builders than God. Each group thought it was better than any of the others.

A huge noise replaced their talking. It made no sense. Everyone was babbling.

Soon the tower fell down by itself, so it was called "the Tower of Babel."

The language of the people of the earth was shattered and broke into pieces. Each one was beautiful, but it was only a piece of the old way of talking together.

Thousands of years passed.

Jesus was born and lived, did his work, and then died on the cross. But that was not the end of the story, because somehow he was still with the people around him as he is with us.

They kept seeing him, and they couldn't let him go. Then one day something amazing happened.

Movements

Place all the symbols of the Twelve, except the symbol for Matthias (the symbol with a sword and book), inside the felt square (the Upper Room).

Move the symbols for the disciples outside the Upper Room and place them in a circle.

With your palms turned up, raise your hands upward together.

Then move the shields (disciples) back inside of the Upper Room.

Add the symbol of Matthias to the group, which is now inside the Upper Room.

Move them outside of the Upper Room.

Words

The disciples were in Jerusalem. Here they are:

Peter, James, John, Andrew, Philip, Bartholomew, Matthew, Thomas, James the Less, Simon, and Jude. There are only eleven disciples because Judas had already died.

Jesus took them outside of Jerusalem to a mountain nearby called "Olivet."

Jesus then went up . . .

and soon the Holy Spirit would come down.

The eleven disciples went back into the city to wait. They were full of joy and went to the Temple to pray.

They then went to the Upper Room and, with God's help, decided that Matthias would take Judas' place.

On Sunday the Twelve were together again. Suddenly there was a sound like a mighty wind rushing in to be with them. It was the Holy Spirit. They became so full of its power that they seemed to be on fire. Their tongues burned in their mouths. They ran down into the street to tell the story.

They were so excited that people wondered what was going on. There were people there from many different countries. They spoke many different languages, but everyone could understand what they were saying.

Movements	Words
	Everyone could see that the Twelve had come close to God—and God had come close to them—in a new way.
	The disciples had become apostles. They went out into all the world to tell the story of Jesus and God's love.
Move the shields (now apostles) out of "Jerusalem" and spread them out all along the edge of the underlay facing out.	
	That was the first Christian Pentecost, but that is not the end of the story, because it is still happening. Wherever people have the courage and power to tell the story, Pentecost is still happening. It is like fire.
Sit back. Collect yourself. Breathe. Then begin the wondering.	
	Now I wonder what part of this story you like best?
	I wonder what the most important part could be?
	I wonder where you are in the story? What part of the story is about you?
	I wonder if we can leave out any part of this story and still have all the story we need?
	I wonder if you have ever come close to something like this?
	I wonder if there is anything in our church that reminds you of this?
When the wondering draws to a close, place everything back in the box. Take the box back to its shelf.	
	Now watch carefully how I put the story away. While I am putting it away, begin thinking about what you are going to get out for your work today.
Help the children choose their work.	

Movements

Words

I wonder what your work will be today? You might make something about this story, or another story that you know. Maybe you want to work on something else.

There are so many things you can choose from. Only you know what is right for you.

Lesson 17

Saul Changes
The Road to Damascus (Acts: 9:1–22)

How to Use This Lesson

- Core Presentation
- Sacred Story: The stories of how God and people meet
- As the seventeenth lesson in Volume 4 of *The Complete Guide to Godly Play* this story is usually presented after the Feast of Pentecost.
- It is part of a comprehensive approach to Christian formation that consists of eight volumes. Together the lessons form a spiral curriculum that enables children to move into adolescence with an inner working knowledge of the classical Christian language system to sustain them all their lives.

The Material

- Location: Sacred Story Shelves (New Testament Shelves)
- Pieces: Wooden tray, red road, two blocks of wood to represent the cities of Jerusalem and Damascus, a wooden plaque with an illustration of the event on the road to Damascus
- Underlay: Tan felt (rectangular shape, approximately thirty-six inches by twenty-four inches or ninety-one by sixty-one centimeters)

Background

Damascus is about 135 miles (217 kilometers) northeast of Jerusalem. Jerusalem is about 2,582 feet (787 meters) and Damascus is about 1,998 feet (609 meters) in elevation, so we can say Saul went from Jerusalem "down" to Damascus. This suggests "The Parable of the Good Samaritan," in which the characters travel from Jerusalem down to Jericho. Another connection is with the light and dark of the first plaque for "The Days of Creation," but this is not evident in the material. These and other connections are not mentioned but left for the children to discover on their own or to be explored by side-by-sides.

The cities and the road are put on the underlay. The storyteller places the transformation card on the road between the two cities when the story comes to the moment when Saul is blinded, going from ordinary light, to darkness, to extraordinary light for living his days.

Saul was one of the first people to know Jesus in "a new way." The disciples saw Jesus in "a new way" at Pentecost in Jerusalem and later outside of

Jerusalem when he ascended. They also saw him in this new way in Galilee when he appeared to them there. Cleopas and his companion met Jesus in this new way on the road to Emmaus. And that is how we meet him today. It might be interesting for older children to find these moments in the Acts of the Apostles in the Bible and in their own lives.

Notes on the Material

The primary material is a plaque with an illustration of what is on the "Road to Damascus" card, which will also be used in the Paul's Travels and His Letters (*Volume 4*, Lesson 18) which extends this lesson by adding more material about where Paul traveled after his transformation and his work of writing letters. It is placed on an underlay that has a wooden block for Jerusalem ("This is Jerusalem.") and another one for Damascus ("This is the city of Damascus."). A red felt road connects the two blocks to represent the road between the two cities. This material has its own tray and is placed on the top shelf of the New Testament Sacred Story Shelves to the right of the story of Jesus and the Twelve (*Volume 4*, Lesson 11). The Extension Lesson, Paul's Travels and His Letters (*Volume 4*, Lesson 18) is placed on the shelf directly below it, with the basket of letters beside it.

Special Notes

An enrichment material for this story is a collection of pictures from the history of art about this moment in the life of Paul. There are many famous examples, but Caravaggio's version is, perhaps, the most dramatic. Additional examples can be downloaded from "Images for Paul's Conversion in Art."[4] Godly Play mentors could download, print, and then laminate them for the children to view. This resource is for older children, who are already grounded in the story itself. Individual mentors need to make this enrichment themselves. Please respect copyrights when making these materials for your private use. It can be placed below the Extension Lesson, Paul's Travels and His Letters (*Volume 4*, Lesson 18).

---

4 www.textweek.com/art/conversion_of_paul.htm (accessed July 13, 2017).

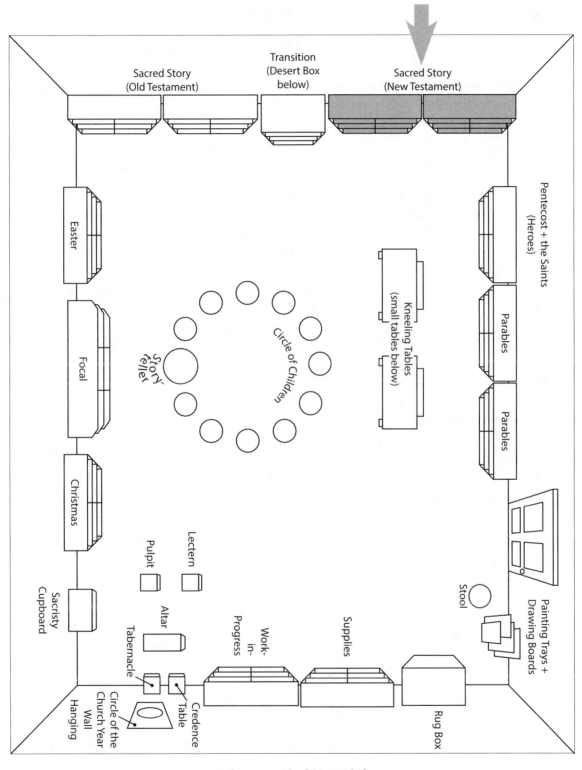

Where to Find Materials

Movements

Go to the New Testament Sacred Story Shelves to get the material for the story. It is on the top shelf next to the story of the Twelve.

Unfold the underlay.

Place the blocks on the underlay (one on each side) and then the road in between.

Point to Jerusalem and then Damascus.

Put down the wooden plaque with the picture of Saul's conversion experience on the road in between Jerusalem and Damascus.

Words

Watch carefully where I go so you will always know where to find this lesson.

Here is Jerusalem. Here is Damascus. Here is the road to Damascus.

There was once someone who went from Jerusalem down to Damascus to bring back as many Christians as he could find to be punished. In those days Christians were called "Followers of the Way."

As Saul went along his way toward Damascus, he was suddenly struck by an intense, terrifying light.

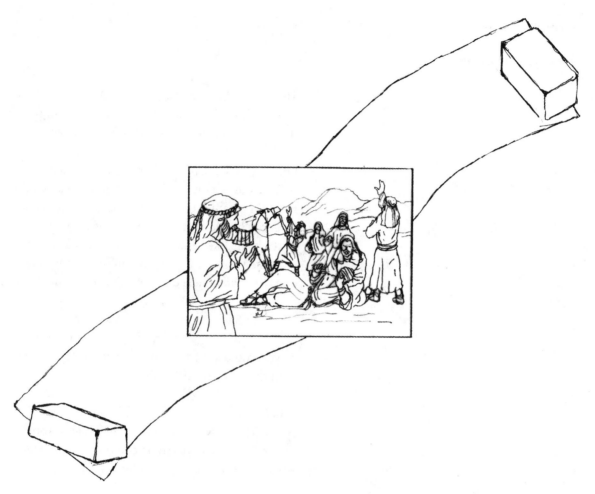

Saul's Conversion Experience (Children's Perspective)

Movements

Pause and look at the picture. Then say:

Words

It blinded him and he fell to the ground.

In his darkness he heard a voice. "Saul, Saul, why are you trying to hurt me?"

"Who are you?"

"I am Jesus, the One you are trying to hurt. Rise up and enter the city. You will be told what to do."

Saul got up and opened his eyes, but he could not see anything. The people with him realized that he was blind so they led him into the city.

Movements

Move the plaque to the city and then put it back on the tray.

Words

They took him to a place on Straight Street, where he stayed for three days. He could not eat anything or even drink water. Mostly he lay on a bed.

One day Saul heard another voice in his darkness. It was Ananias, a Follower of the Way. God had told Ananias to go to Straight Street to meet Saul, but he didn't want to. Saul was trying to hurt people like him, but Ananias went anyway. Now he was standing in front of his enemy, the one who had attacked other Followers of the Way.

"Brother, Saul, it was the Lord Jesus who appeared to you on the road. He sent me to you so you could see again and so you could be filled with the Holy Spirit."

Saul listened very carefully and then he understood. That is when something like scales from a fish fell from his eyes so he could see again. He stood up. Ananias baptized him.

That is when Saul changed and became new again. He began to eat and drink once more and became a Follower of the Way.

Saul was one of the first people to know Jesus in this new way. It changed him, so he changed his name from Saul to Paul, which is how we still know him.

Sit quietly for a moment and then begin the wondering.

I wonder what part of this story you liked the best?

I wonder what part was the most important?

I wonder what part was about you or what part you were in?

Movements

Put the blocks back on the tray. Fold up the road and place it on the tray. Fold the under-lay and put it on the tray. Return the materials to the shelf.

Return to your storytelling spot and begin to help the children choose work for the day.

Words

I wonder if there is any part of the story that we could leave out and still have all that we need?

Watch how I put the story away.

I wonder what your work will be today? You might make something about this story, or another story that you know. Maybe you want to work with something else. There are so many things you can choose from. Only you know what is right for you.

Paul's Travels and His Letters

Living in the Power of the Holy Spirit

How to Use This Lesson

- Extension Story
- Sacred Story: The stories of how God and people meet
- "Extensions" extend the Core Lessons. They expand not only Sacred Stories but also the Liturgical and Parable lessons. Extension Lessons sit on the shelves below the Core Lessons, which are displayed on the top shelf in the Godly Play room. This lesson extends *Saul Changes* (*Volume 4*, Lesson 17).
- As the eighteenth lesson in Volume 4 of *The Complete Guide to Godly Play* it is usually presented after the children are familiar with *Saul Changes* (*Volume 4*, Lesson 17), and after the Day of Pentecost.
- It is part of a comprehensive approach to Christian formation that consists of eight volumes. Together the lessons form a spiral curriculum that enables children to move into adolescence with an inner working knowledge of the classical Christian language system to sustain them all their lives.

The Material

- Location: Sacred Story (New Testament Shelves)
- Pieces: Wooden tray, seven wooden plaques illustrated with scenes of Paul's life, thirteen letter scrolls, map of Paul's travels
- Underlay: Red strip of felt

Background

The Holy Spirit continues Jesus' presence beyond his historical life. Paul discovered this on the road to Damascus and elaborated his thinking about what happened to him in his letters. He knew Jesus in a new way, quite different from the way the disciples knew Jesus. The Holy Spirit draws aside a curtain so we can be "in," "with," and "of" Christ, who has been there all the time, waiting to be found and to find us.

This lesson presents the story of Paul's discovering the power of the Holy Spirit. The narrative is important in itself, but it is also one that can be connected to the Creator (see *The Complete Guide to Godly Play*, *Volume 2*, Lesson 4) and Christ (see *The Complete Guide to Godly Play*, *Volume 4*, Lessons 2–8). The Holy Trinity is a Synthesis Lesson (see *The Complete Guide to Godly Play*, *Volume 4*, Lesson 19) that provides a narrative introduction to the dynamic concept and symbol of the Holy Trinity. This ancient and powerful view of God challenges us to be more sensitive to the complexity of God's elusive presence.

In the beginning of Acts, Luke tells us that just before his ascension, Jesus responded to the disciples' question about the restoration of the kingdom by saying, "It is not for you to know the times or periods that the Father has set by his own authority. But you will receive power when the Holy Spirit has come upon you; and you will be my witnesses in Jerusalem, in all Judea and Samaria, and to the ends of the earth" (Acts 1:7–8). Paul was one of the witnesses who went to the "ends of the earth" in the power of the Holy Spirit.

Notes on the Material

Find this material on the second shelf of the New Testament Shelves beneath "Saul Changes" (*Volume 4*, Lesson 17). A wooden tray holds:

- Thirteen letter scrolls, one for each of Paul's New Testament letters
- The rolled-up red underlay
- Seven wood plaques with illustrations of the following seven moments in Paul's life:

  1. Leaving Tarsus
  2. Studying at the Temple
  3. Experience on the Road to Damascus (This plaque can be found on the shelf above with the materials for "Saul Changes" (*Volume 4*, Lesson 17).
  4. Escape from Damascus
  5. Letters to the New Churches
  6. Jerusalem for the Last Time
  7. Paul's Death

- A map showing Paul's travels

The Seven Paul Plaques and their Sources

The New Testament story of Paul is found primarily in the Acts of the Apostles, which tells the story from Pentecost through Paul's final days in Rome. The narrative begins with Peter, and Paul doesn't appear until the stoning of Stephen in 7:58. From then on, Paul takes over the story. The following seven moments tempt the child to know more:

1. **Leaving Tarsus (Paul's birth)**

   Paul refers to his birth in the speech he made to the angry mob on his last journey to Jerusalem. See Acts 22:3.

2. **Studying at the Temple**

   In the same speech in Jerusalem, Paul also referred to having been a student of Gamaliel. See Acts 22:3.

3. **Experience on the Road to Damascus (Baptism by the Holy Spirit)**

   The story of Paul's encounter with Jesus' presence on the road to Damascus occurs early in Acts (see 9:1–19). He refers to this event twice more, once in his speech to the angry mob in Jerusalem (Acts 22:6–16) and again during his defense before King Agrippa (26:12–18). This plaque is used in the Core Lesson about Paul entitled, "Saul Changes" (*Volume 4*, Lesson 17). You will bring both materials to the circle when you present this lesson on Paul's Travels and Letters.

4. **Escape from Damascus (and Paul's time in the desert)**

   The escape from Damascus appears in Acts 9:23–25. Paul refers to it in 2 Corinthians 11:32–33 and briefly notes his time in the desert of Arabia in Galatians 1:17.

5. **Letters to the New Churches (Paul's work: telling about the power of the Holy Spirit and writing letters)**

   Paul's missionary journeys are primarily found in the Acts of the Apostles:

   - First Journey, Acts 13:1–14, 28
   - The Jerusalem Conference, Acts 15:1–35
   - Second Journey, Acts 15:36–18:22
   - Third Journey, Acts 18:23–21:16

   The letters of Paul are not literary, like those of Aristotle, Epicurus, or Paul's contemporary Seneca, a Roman who wrote "moral epistles." Nor are they personal, like most of the papyrus letters from the first and second centuries. Paul's letters are somewhere between, meant to be read aloud and passed among congregations. We still follow this tradition when we read and discuss these letters in church.

This lesson uses the New Testament collection of Paul's letters. Not all scholars are convinced that he was the author of all the thirteen letters that bear his name. The debate over Pauline authorship is not our focus here, but here are the unquestioned and questioned Pauline writings:

Unquestioned

1 Thessalonians
Galatians
Philippians
Philemon
1 Corinthians
2 Corinthians
Romans

Questioned

2 Thessalonians
Colossians
Ephesians
Titus (pastoral letter)
1 Timothy (pastoral letter)
2 Timothy (pastoral letter)

The questioned writings might have been written by disciples of Paul, who saw themselves as speaking for him and continuing his presence in the Church. For a well-balanced treatment of this issue, please see Chapter 25 of Raymond E. Brown's *An Introduction to the New Testament* (New York: Doubleday, 1997).

6. Jerusalem for the Last Time

Paul's final journey to Jerusalem resulted in his becoming a prisoner of the Romans. He was then moved to the coast, to Caesarea, and finally sailed to Rome by way of Crete and Malta to be tried in the Roman courts, as was his right as a Roman citizen. See Acts 2:17–28:31.

7. Paul's Death (death and yet . . .)

The known chronology of Paul's life begins sometime after Jesus' death about 30 CE. If it took about two years for the events of Acts 1–8 to take place, then Paul's conversion happened about 32 CE. By 60–62 CE, we find him in Rome under house arrest.

Legend takes over where Acts ends. Paul was probably executed in Rome during the rule of Nero, who dies by his own hand on June 9, 68. Paul may have lived in Rome during the years between his house arrest and death, or he may have gone to Spain for a time and returned to his death.

As a Roman citizen, Paul was probably executed by sword or an ax. (Non-citizens were killed by burning, in the games, or by crucifixion.) Where did he die? There are two traditions: One is based on the legend that Paul's head bounced three times after it was severed from his body, resulting in three springs that started flowing at each spot where it touch the earth. This place is called, appropriately, *Tre Fontane* ("Three Fountains"). The other tradition holds that the location of his death and burial is the spot where Constantine built a basilica around 324. Today that church is called "St. Paul's" Outside the Walls in Rome. Another tradition links these two sites: A person named Lucina was said to have carried Paul's remains from *Tre Fontane*, where he was killed, to his burial place at St. Paul's Outside the Walls.

Special Notes

As in the Creation story, you will lay the cards out on a strip moving from your right to left, so the children can "read" the story being laid out from their left to right.

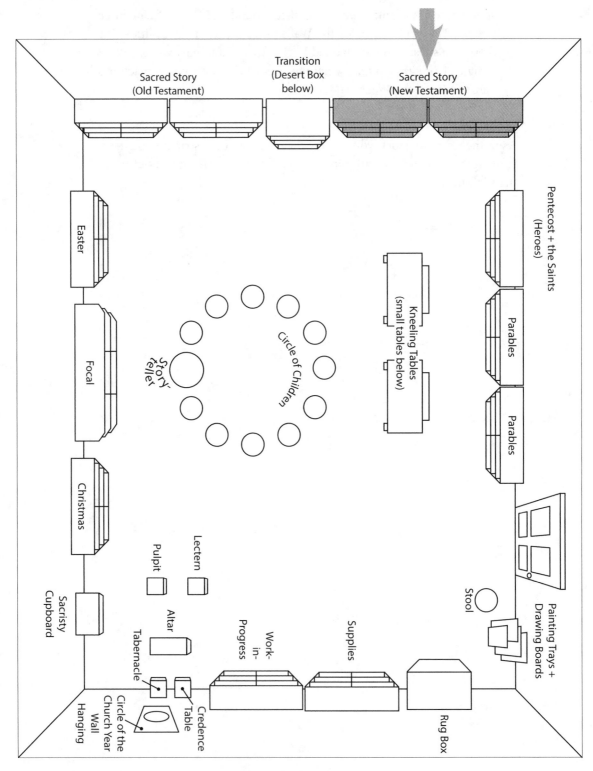

Where to Find Materials

Movements

When the children are settled, go and get the material. As you stand beside the New Testament shelves, point to the tray that holds the materials to tell the story of Paul's Travels.

Bring the tray of materials for the story, "Saul Changes" (Volume 4, Lesson 17) to the circle. Return to the shelves and get the tray of materials for Paul's Travels.

Settle yourself back in your spot. Place one tray to your right and the other to your left. Then pick up the red underlay.

Leaving Tarsus (Paul's birth)
Unroll the red underlay far enough to your left so there is a space for the first card. Pick up the first card and hold it as you begin.

Words

Watch carefully where I go so you will always know where to find this material.

Today I want to share the story of Paul's travels with you. But to do that, I also need this lesson about how he was changed. I think I will need to take two trips.

In the beginning the baby was born. His mother and father named him Saul after the first king of Israel. His home was in a city called "Tarsus," near the sea.

As the boy grew, he helped his father in his shop. Saul's father made tents. Even though Saul's family lived far from Rome and were Jewish, they were made Roman citizens like many others in the city. Perhaps this had something to do with making tents for the Roman army.

Saul heard many languages in the streets of Tarsus, but it was the language of the synagogue he loved most. His father and he read the Torah together. Saul was very serious about knowing the Hebrew Bible.

Movements

Words

Saul grew. When it was time, he decided to go to the great city of Jerusalem, so he could have the best of all the teachers. He waved goodbye to his family and home in Tarsus and traveled to the holy city.

Place the first card, "Leaving Tarsus," on the underlay, facing the children.

Studying at the Temple
Unroll the red underlay far enough so there is space for the second card, "Studying at the Temple." Pick up the card and hold it as you tell the next part of the story.

When Saul entered the city through a great high gate, he went first to the Temple. He worshiped there. That is probably also where he studied and worked. His teacher was Gamaliel, or another rabbi in Gamaliel's family. Saul wanted to be one of the Pharisees, who worked hard to understand and keep all the laws in the Torah.

Saul worked hard to understand and keep the laws. He had no time or patience for people who did not. One day he heard about the Followers of the Way. They thought that the Messiah had come. It was Jesus of Nazareth.

When Saul heard that, he became angry. The Messiah was supposed to drive away the Roman soldiers and rule with justice and mercy. Jesus was a criminal who was crucified. Besides, in the Law it says that God curses any criminal who is "hanged upon a tree." These people were telling lies about God. He had to stop them from saying such things.

Stephen was one of the most important of the Followers of the Way. The priests in the Temple decided to punish him.

Movements

Place the card so that it touches the first card.

Experience on the Road to Damascus (Baptism by the Holy Spirit)
Unroll the red underlay far enough so there is a space for the third card "Experience on the Road to Damascus" Pick up the card from the Core Lesson "Saul Changes"(Volume 4, Lesson 17) and hold it as you tell the next part of the story.

Place the card so that it touches the card in the second position.

Words

He was taken outside the city walls to be killed. Saul held the coats of the ones who threw stones at Stephen until he died. Then Saul was given a letter by the High Priest to go to Damascus to catch more Followers of the Way and bring them back to Jerusalem for punishment.

Saul traveled to Damascus.

You have heard this part of the story. Remember how one afternoon he climbed up the road toward the city. Suddenly there was a great light! It was so bright that he fell to the ground. He could see nothing.

In his darkness a voice came to him: "Saul, Saul, why are you trying to hurt me? Why are you persecuting me?"

All Saul could say was, "Who are you, Lord?"

The voice answered, "I am Jesus, the One you are persecuting. Get up. Go into the city. You will be told what to do."

Saul tried to get up. He looked for the path, but he was blind.

Saul was led into the city and left at a house on Straight Street.

Movements

Escape from Damascus (and Paul's time in the Desert)
Unroll the red underlay far enough so there is space for the fourth card, "Escape from Damascus." Pick up the fourth card and hold it as you tell the next part of the story.

Words

For three days he went without food or water. Then, in the chaos and the darkness of his blindness, he heard another voice. "Hello, brother Saul, I am Ananias. I was sent by Jesus to lay hands on you and bless you."

When Ananias' hands touched Saul, something like the scales from a fish fell from his eyes and he could see. Then Ananias baptized him. Saul was changed forever. He could feel the power of the Holy Spirit growing inside of him. Then Ananias and Saul ate together.

Slowly Saul regained his strength. When he was better, he went to the synagogue to tell his fellow Jews the good news about what had happened to him. When they heard what Saul said, they tried to kill him. They even put guards at the city gate to catch him if he tried to get away, but Followers of the Way hid Saul in the city and they couldn't find him.

One night when it was dark, Saul and a small group of the Followers of the Way climbed quietly to the top of the city wall. They carried a large basket and lots of rope. They tied the rope to the basket, and Saul climbed inside. They lowered him down the wall and he disappeared into the dark.

Saul went into the desert of Arabia. He was confused and needed to understand what God wanted him to do. He had come to Damascus to catch Followers of the Way, but now he was one of them. What did this mean?

Movements

Place the card so that it touches the third card.

Letters to New Churches (Paul's work: telling about the power of the Holy Spirit and writing letters)

Unroll the red underlay far enough so there is a space for the fifth card. Pick up the fifth card and hold it as you tell the next part of the story.

Words

Saul prayed. He watched the empty desert and listened to its silence. He came so close to God and God came so close to him that he knew what God wanted him to do.

He was to travel to the ends of the earth and tell people what had happened to him. His work was to try to say how his hate had turned into love and to begin churches where people could show how this was done. He also was to write letters to help new churches do this.

Saul began his work. He sailed across the sea. He walked across the land.

He went back to Jerusalem to meet with Peter, James, and the others there, now called "Christians." They were suspicious, but they finally said to keep telling the story to the Gentiles, the non-Jews.

Saul even changed his name. He was traveling so much in the Roman Empire that he began to use his Roman name, "Paul."

Paul's work was to start churches, but he also wrote letters to young churches to help them with their problems. He wrote to the Philippians and the Ephesians. He wrote to the Thessalonians and the Corinthians. He even wrote to the Romans and told them he wanted to visit them and then go on to Spain.

Movements

Place the fifth card, "Letters to the New Churches," so that it touches the fourth card.

Jerusalem for the Last Time
Unroll the red underlay far enough so there is a space for the sixth card, "Jerusalem for the Last Time." Pick up the sixth card and hold it as you tell the next part of the story.

Words

Paul turned toward Jerusalem for the last time. As soon as he came into the city he went to the Temple. He wanted to make a sacrifice. He was still a Nazarite, keeping strict Jewish Law, as well as being a Christian.

People shouted that he didn't belong there. Some began to push him. The Roman soldiers came running. They pushed the people back with their shields, short swords, and spears. They saved Paul's life and marched him to the Fortress Antonia.

The Roman soldiers decided to beat him to find out why the Jews wanted to kill him, but that was when Paul told them he was a Roman citizen. He had to be taken to the Roman courts.

He was taken to Caesarea on the coast. After about two years he was put on a ship that was sailing to Rome to be judged in the law courts there.

Place the sixth card so that it touches the fifth card.

Paul's Death (Death and yet . . .)

Unroll the red underlay far enough so there is a space for the seventh card. Pick up the last card and hold it as you tell this part of the story.

Movements

Words

Paul sailed to Rome. His ship sank, but he was saved and went on anyway.

Paul was kept a prisoner in his own house. A soldier guarded him, but he could go visit friends while he was waiting for the Roman court to decide what he had done wrong.

Some say that Paul went on to Spain and then came back to Rome. Others think he was executed after the great fire, which burned Rome in the year 67. I like to think of Paul as still traveling on "to the ends of the earth."

Place the seventh card, "Paul's Death," so that it touches the sixth card.

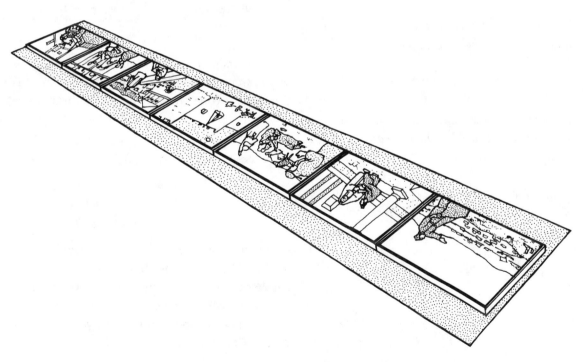

The Seven Cards on the Underlay (Storyteller's Perspective)

I wonder

Movements

Place all thirteen letter scrolls on the last card.

Sit back and enjoy the story of Paul as it is laid out.

You then begin the wondering.

Pick up the map of Paul's travels from the tray and unroll it facing the children.

Slowly return everything back on the trays, modeling for the children how to care for the materials.

Return the two trays to the New Testament Shelves and then help the children choose their work.

Words

Paul's work was to tell his story and to write letters. He became a story himself, and his letters are still being read in churches to this very day.

Now I wonder what part of this story you like best?

I wonder what part is the most important part?

I wonder what part of this story is about you?

I wonder if there is any part of the story we can leave out and still have all the story we need?

Here is a map of Paul's travels. He started in Jerusalem, went to Damascus. See you can follow his travels with your finger by following this red line.

I wonder what your work will be today? You might make something about this story, or another story that you know. Maybe you want to work on something else. There are so many things you can choose from. Only you know what is right for you.

Lesson 19

The Holy Trinity
A strange three-in-one logic

How to Use This Lesson

- Synthesis Lesson: Godly Play teaches children the art of how to make meaning with four key genres of the Christian language system: Parables, Sacred Stories, Liturgical Action, and Contemplative Silence. The Synthesis Lesson for the Sacred Stories pulls together three lessons (the Faces of Easter, Creation, and Paul's Travels and Letters) to transform them into the concept of the Holy Trinity.
- Sacred Story: The stories of how God and people meet
- As the nineteenth lesson in Volume 4 of *The Complete Guide to Godly Play,* it is usually presented to children who are at least nine years old and have had several years of experience with all of the Core Lessons.
- It is part of a comprehensive approach to Christian formation that consists of eight volumes. Together the lessons form a spiral curriculum that enables children to move into adolescence with an inner working knowledge of the classical Christian language system to sustain them all their lives.

The Material

- Location: Sacred Story Shelves, Lent/Easter Shelf Unit, Focal Shelf Unit
- Pieces: Creation materials; Faces of Easter materials; Paul's Travels and Letters; three white circles from Baptism materials (see Notes on the Material, below, for full listings)
- Underlay: None

Background

Through the Sacred Stories, we have followed God's elusive presence. In the fourth century, the People of God discovered yet another way to understand this experience. It was by a strange three-in-one logic. The stories in which God, Jesus, and the Holy Spirit were characters were somehow one story, and yet distinct. This way of thinking preserved the unique aspects of the stories, yet joined them as one.

The Holy Trinity's inner communication is unknown to us. This is because we are created beings, made by God. We can only guess about this inner communication from what we know about how we experience God's relationship with us. As Catherine Mowry LaCugna has powerfully argued in *God for Us* (San Francisco: Harper San Francisco, 1973), "the doctrine of the Trinity is ultimately therefore a teaching not about the abstract nature of God, nor about God in isolation from everything other than God, but a teaching about God's life with us and our life with each other" (p. 1).

This lesson combines three narratives, transforming them into the concept of the Holy Trinity. That's exactly what happened in the history of the Church in the fourth century. Under the pressure of Greek philosophy, the Church integrated three narratives, like the ones in this lesson, and developed its three-in-one logic to make them one and yet keep them distinct.

Notes on the Material

The materials for this lesson are three stories told with wooden plaques. Two of the stories are found in *Volume 4*: the Faces of Easter (Lessons 2–8) and Paul's Travels and Letters—which includes the material used for the Core Lesson on Paul entitled, "Saul Changes" (*Volume 4*, Lessons 17 and 18). The third story, "Creation," is found in *Volume 2* (Lesson 4). Each of these three stories is grouped into seven units, as shown here:

Faces of Easter

1. Jesus' Birth and Growth

2. Jesus is Lost and Found

3. Jesus' Baptism and Blessing by God

4. Jesus' Desert and Discovery Experience

5. Jesus as Healer and Parable-Maker

6. Jesus Offers the Bread and Wine

7. The One who was Easter and Still is

Days of Creation

1. Light and Dark

2. Water

3. Dry Land and Growing Things

4. Day and Night

5. Swimming and Flying

6. Creatures that Walk

7. Rest and Remember

Paul's Travels & Letters

1. Leaving Tarsus (Paul's Birth)

2. Studying at the Temple

3. Experience on the Road to Damascus (Baptism by the Holy Spirit)

4. Escape from Damascus (from "Saul Changes" (*Volume 4*, Lesson 17)

5. Letters to the Churches (Paul's work: Telling about the Power of the Holy Spirit and Writing Letters)

6. Jerusalem for the Last Time

7. Paul's Death (Death and Yet . . .)

Finally, you will need, from the Holy Baptism lesson (*Volume 3*, Lesson 8), the three white circles. You will lay these circles, the symbol of the Trinity, over the curious "mess" we will have created and begin to wonder about the ways God relates to us, the ways we relate to God, and the ways God relates to God within the communion of the Trinity itself.

Special Notes

Because this lesson pulls together three stories through the means of a fourth lesson (Holy Baptism), we suggest its use only with older children who are already familiar with the stories of Creation, Holy Baptism, the Faces of Easter, and Paul's Travels and Letters (which includes the material from the Core Lesson about Paul entitled "Saul Changes" (*Volume 4*, Lesson 17). You, too, will need to be familiar with these presentations to tell this Synthesis Lesson. The directions given below will tell you only how to adjust the basic presentations for this Synthesis Lesson.

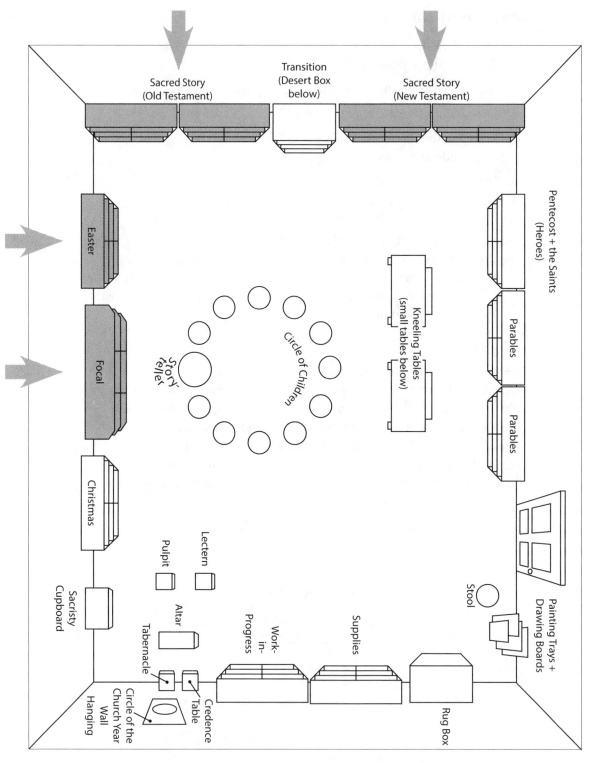

Where to Find Materials

Movements

When the children are settled, go and get the materials for the Faces of Easter, Creation, and Paul's Travels and Letters (including the materials for the Core Lesson—Saul Changes).

Place the materials for two of the presentations on one side of you, and the materials for the other two presentations on the other side of you.

Wait for the children to settle, and then begin.

First lay out the Faces of Easter vertically (see the illustrations in Volume 4, page 186), so the life of Jesus grows away from you toward the children in the circle. Name each "Face" saying:

Then move the Faces into a circle (see Faces of Easter VII, Lesson 8, Volume 4, p. 80 for instructions), leaving room at the top of the circle to place the Creation underlay.

Sit back and look at the lesson. Then say:

Unroll the black underlay for Creation. Then lay the wooden plaques out, naming the days of Creation. Each time you say that God said,

Words

Watch carefully where I go so you will always know where to find this material.

There's a lot, isn't there?

First we remember when the baby was born. Then we remember how Jesus was lost and then found. Then we remember Jesus' Baptism and blessing by God. Then we remember how Jesus went into the desert to discover more about who he was and what his work was going to be. Then we remember how his work was to heal people and make Parables. Then we remember how he went to Jerusalem for the last time, became a Parable, and offered the bread and the wine. And here is how we remember how he became Easter and still is.

You know this lesson. You have seen it before, but there is always more. Now let me show you something interesting.

Movements

"It is good," rest your hand on the card gently as a kind of blessing. See illustration, Volume 2, page 71 to see how to lay the story out.

Words

On the first day God gave us the gift of light and God said, "It is good." On the second day God gave us water and God said, "It is good." On the third day God gave us the dry land and the green and growing things and God said, "It is good." On the fourth day God gave us the day and the night and God said, "It is good." On the fifth day God gave us the creatures that swim and the creatures that fly and God said, "It is good." On the sixth day God gave us the creatures that walk upon the earth and God said, "It is very good." On the seventh day God gave us the day to rest and remember all of the gifts of the other days.

Creation and The Faces of Easter (Children's Perspective)

Movements

When you finish laying out the Creation story, omit the wondering questions. Instead invite the children to combine the two lessons as follows:

Pause a moment. Look at the Creation and the Faces of Easter. Speak slowly and with wonder.

Pick up the first Creation plaque that shows "light." Look at it, then look directly at the children.

Don't place the plaque down without direction from the children. Only if they have no suggestions would you offer an example by picking a place that seems right to you on that day.

As you respond to the children's suggestions, there are several queries you can make, for example:

Let the children make their own decisions about such questions of placement. Affirm and support the children's choices, including the choice of diverse ideas.

After all the Creation plaques are placed with the Face Cards plaques, roll up the underlay and place it to the side. Then say:

Unroll the red underlay for Paul's Travels and Letters above the other lessons. Lay out the plaques, saying something about each one.

Words

Hmm. Look at this.

I wonder where this day goes in that story?

Let's try this.

Shall I put the card here? Should I place it beside or above? Below? Do they need to be touching? Do you want it to also touch this other card? Shall I turn it like this?

Those are all wonderful ideas. I'm just going to place the card here, so we can go on. When you work with this on your own or with a friend, you can put it anywhere you want to.

Now let me show you something else.

In the beginning Saul was born. He grew and when it was time he left home.

Saul went to Jerusalem to study at the Temple.

Movements	Words
	On the road to Damascus he met Jesus in a new way.
	He went into the desert to discover who he was and what his work was going to be.
	His work was to start churches and to write letters.
	He went to Jerusalem for the last time.
	He finally went to Rome where he died, but is still alive today through his letters.
Look back and forth between the story you have just presented and the two stories integrated together.	
Pick up the first Paul plaque and say:	
	I wonder where this card goes in those stories?
	I wonder where these cards go in those stories? Hmm. Here is Paul studying in the Temple. Here he is on the Road to Damascus.
Repeat this with each plaque. Again, place the plaques according to the children's suggestions. Ask questions to clarify their directions.	
Finally, you will have guided the placing of all the Paul story with the Faces and with the days of Creation. Roll up the red underlay and place it to the side. Sit back again. Look at the clutter.	
	What a curious "mess"! What shall we do? It is all mixed up.
Reach behind you to get the three white circles from the Baptism Lesson on the Focal Shelf Unit. Leave them rolled up for a moment.	
	This is the Baptism lesson. We don't need all of it. Let's just take these three circles.
Unroll and smooth out each one as you place it over the mixed-up plaques. Form three connecting circles that cover as much of the plaques as possible. Smooth out each circle as you name it.	

Movements	Words
	When we baptize people we baptize them in "the name of the Father, and of the Son, and of the Holy Spirit."

The Holy Trinity (Children's Perspective)

Movements

Sit back and look at what you have done.

Touch one of the circles.

Touch each circle again.

Sit back again. Then begin the wondering.

.

You can wonder, too, about how God relates to God within the Trinity. This is presumptuous wondering, but many great theologians like Thomas Aquinas have wondered about this before us.

Words

There, that's better.

Now the stories are all connected by the circles, and yet each one is still there by itself. This is a strange kind of three-in-one thinking.

You see? They are all connected and yet each one is still there. It just isn't by itself anymore.

This is a symbol for the Holy Trinity.

It is the Father, the Son, and the Holy Spirit; one God and yet still three stories about God. We know each story tells something different and yet they are still all together at the same time. That's the three-in-one thinking.

Now I wonder which one of the three-in-one ways you like best to come close to God?

I wonder which one of the three-in-one ways is the most important way to come close to God?

I wonder which one of the three-in-one ways is most like the way you come close to God most easily? Which one is the most natural for you?

I wonder which one of the three-in-one ways we can leave out and still have all the ways we need?

I wonder which one of the three-in-one ways God likes best to be with God?

I wonder which one of the three-in-one ways God knows is the most important way to be with God?

Movements	Words
	I wonder which one of the three-in-one ways is the way God most easily and naturally is with God?
	I wonder if God can leave out any of the three-in-one ways to be with God and still have all the ways God needs to be God?
	Remember you don't have to hurry. Look at all of this. I really do wonder how these stories fit together? I wonder how they are one and yet three? It is easy to see that they are, but it's hard to talk about, isn't it? God is not so simple and yet God is, and that is truly wonderful.
When the wondering loses its energy, you can then begin to put the lesson back into its various trays and baskets. Show all of this putting away to the children so they will not feel as if they have to hurry. It is a lot to put away, but you want to show that you are still involved with all the parts of the synthesis as well as the whole.	
	Remember to be thinking about what work you are going to get out while I am putting all of this away. It's a lot, isn't it? There.
After everything is put away, begin to help the children choose their own work.	
	Now, I wonder what work you would like to get out today? It could be something about the Trinity, or it could be about something else. There are so many things you can choose from. Only you know what is right for you.

Lesson 20

The Part That Hasn't Been Written Yet

What will happen next?

How to Use This Lesson

- Extension Presentation
- Sacred Story: The stories of how God and people meet
- As the twentieth lesson in Volume 4 of *The Complete Guide to Godly Play*, it is usually presented to children who are familiar with the Core Sacred Stories in a Godly Play Room.
- "Extensions" extend the Core Lessons. They extend not only Sacred Stories but also the Liturgical Action and Parable lessons. Extension Lessons generally sit on the shelves below the Core Lessons, which are displayed on the top shelf in the Godly Play room. This lesson extends the Books of the Bible (Volume 2, pages 47–54) and really all of the Sacred Stories so it is placed at the very end of the New Testament shelves.
- It is part of a comprehensive approach to Christian formation that consists of eight volumes. Together the lessons form a spiral curriculum that enables children to move into adolescence with an inner working knowledge of the classical Christian language system to sustain them all their lives.

The Material

- Location: Sacred Story (New Testament Shelves)
- Pieces: Book stand, blank book (or journal)
- Underlay: None

Background

Even though the Bible is officially complete, the journey with the elusive presence of God continues. We are not sure what will happen in our lifetime. The future is the time of the children.

Notes on the Material

Find this material on the far right of the top shelf of the New Testament Sacred Story Shelves.

The material is a blank book or journal on a book stand. Find or buy a journal and stand that are beautiful, mysterious, and intriguing. You do not plan a time for this presentation. You wait until children ask you about the material before offering this presentation.

Special Notes

Your favorite book store is a good source for beautiful blank journals.

Another possibility would be to borrow a book from the library on making books and to create your own journal.

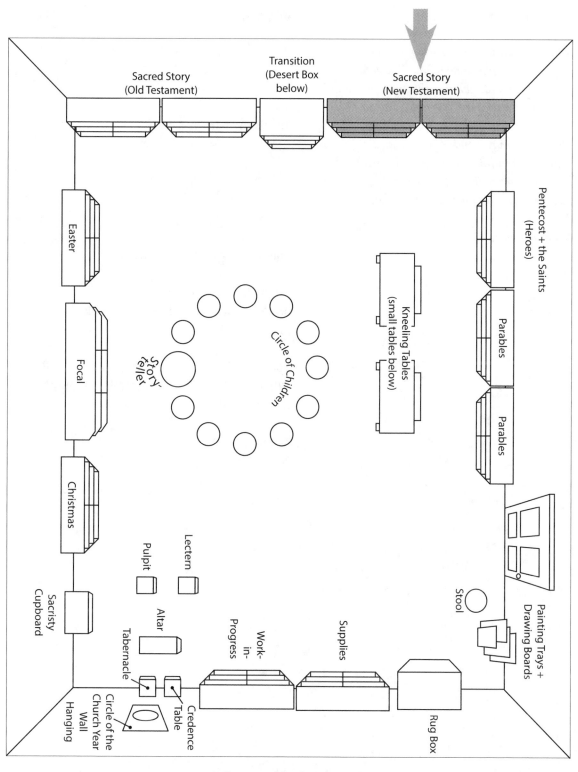

Where to Find Materials

Movements

This presentation begins when a child or a group of children come to you to ask about this strange material, i.e., the book stand and book. They might ask, "What is this for?"

Now you can respond. The italicized questions that follow in this column of movement directions are questions that the children might ask—or that you might suggest yourself.

Who will write it?

What will we do?

Words

This is the part that hasn't been written yet.

You will. I might not be there.

I don't know. That is up to you. What will you do? What will you write in the book about the journey of the People of God with God?

You may write something now or wait until later. When you are finished, remember to put the material back.

Appendix A: The Foundational Literature for Godly Play

The foundational literature for Godly Play is organized by the following themes: the key assumption, an introduction, the historical contexts, the biblical theology, the method, the theory of spiritual guidance, the view of children's spirituality, a sense of maturity, and Godly Play in the home. The literature for these nine themes will now be concisely discussed.

The Key Assumption

Hans Urs von Balthasar, *Unless You Become Like This Child*, 1991.
David Hay, *Something There: The Biology of the Human Spirit*, 2007.
Edward Robinson, *The Original Vision: A Study of the Religious Experience of Childhood*, 1983.

Godly Play assumes that children experience the presence of God at an early age. This means that we don't need to convince them that God exists, but we need to help them better understand what they already know without distorting it. The way to better understand God's presence is to learn classical Christian language to identify the experience of God amid their other experiences, name it, express its richness, evaluate what they know, and use it to make ultimate meaning to guide their lives.

The formal teaching of Christian language needs to begin during early childhood, about three to six years, and continue to be supported during middle childhood, about six to nine years, and late childhood, about nine to twelve years. This will enable children to enter adolescence with an inner working model of the whole Christian language system to use as they create a new, more expanded, and complex identity during their adolescent years.

Theology has not always appreciated that children know God at an early age, but a twentieth century exception was Hans Urs von Balthasar (1905–1988). He thought that the undifferentiated presence of God began to be focused for the child in the mother's smile. His last book, *Unless You Become Like this Child*, emphasized the importance of young children's experience of God and the need for adults to appreciate and learn from this.

Science has also not fully appreciated the spirituality of young children. This has begun to change and David Hay's *Something There: The Biology of the Human Spirit* has helped bring about this change. Hay's book expands and links his thought to that of Alister Hardy, the Head of the Department of Zoology and Comparative Anatomy at Oxford University from 1946–1961. After retirement Hardy founded the Religious Experience Research Unit at Manchester College, Oxford. RERU is now called "the Alister Hardy Religious Experience Research Centre" and is located at the University of Wales, Trinity Saint David. Hay, who died in 2014, also wrote a biography of Alister Hardy called *God's Biologist* (2011). The work of Hardy, Hay, and others has helped overcome the taboo of talking about the experience of God's presence in science. Edward Robinson's *The Original Vision* led the way concerning children. He was the first director of RERU and concentrated on the empirical study of children's experience of God as part of their original vision of reality.

An Introduction to Godly Play

Jerome W. Berryman, *Godly Play: A Way of Religious Education,* 1991.

This book introduces the reader to the theory and practice of Godly Play. It combines developmental psychology and Montessori education with God's presence, theology, play, and the creative process to articulate an approach for mentoring children to become mature Christians.

Godly Play: A Way of Religious Education discusses the ultimate game, the importance of laughter, and the structure of a Godly Play experience. It also discusses six aspects of the spoken and unspoken "lessons" in terms of wonder, community/ethics, the participants' existential limits, the nature of religious language, the importance of associating religious language with the creative process to make existential meaning, and the Holy Eucharist as the deep structure for the Godly Play approach to the spiritual guidance of children (and adults).

The Historical Contexts for Godly Play

Jerome W. Berryman, *Children and the Theologians: Clearing the Way for Grace,* 2009.
E. M. Standing, *The Child in the Church,* 1965.
Jerome W. Berryman, *The Spiritual Guidance of Children: Montessori, Godly Play, and the Future,* 2013.
Brendan Hyde, *The Search for a Theology of Childhood: Essays by Jerome W. Berryman from 1978–2009,* 2013.

The historical context for Godly Play has three levels. *Children and the Theologians: Clearing the Way for Grace* provides the big picture by examining selected theologians' views of children. The themes of a *de facto* doctrine of children emerged from this study. Children are treated with ambivalence, ambiguity, indifference, and grace. This *implied* doctrine still influences us today, so this needs to be acknowledged in a conscious way and an *explicit* alternative needs to be articulated. This book calls for children to be understood as a means of grace.

The second level of historical context is the history of Maria Montessori's interest in children's spirituality. It is important to see how Godly Play fits into the first four generations of Montessori religious education. A collection of primary sources for understanding this history may be found in E. M. Standing's *The Child in the Church*, which includes chapters by Maria Montessori, Standing, Sofia Cavalletti, and others. This history is elaborated in *The Spiritual Guidance of Children: Montessori, Godly Play, and the Future.*

The third historical context is how Godly Play developed in Jerome Berryman's work. Brendan Hyde's book traces the development of Godly Play through published articles. *The Search for a Theology of Childhood: Essays by Jerome W. Berryman from 1978–2009* was published by Connor Court Publishing, in Australia (2013).

The Biblical Theology

Samuel Terrien, *The Elusive Presence: Toward a New Biblical Theology*, 1978.

Terrien writes, "When presence is 'guaranteed' to human senses or reason, it is no longer real presence. The proprietary sight of the glory destroys the vision, whether in the Temple of Zion or in the eucharistic body. . . . In biblical faith, presence eludes but does not delude" (476).

Children know God's elusive presence, but they have few opportunities to learn an adequate language to identify, name, express, or gain perspective on it. Most of the language they learn in school is the language of science, including the social sciences, and outside of school they are taught the language of consumers. Godly Play makes classical Christian language available to them in a way that allows them to discover that what they have experienced personally has important echoes in the larger narrative of the Bible and the church. Organizing the curriculum of Godly Play around the child's journey gives children a sense that what they have experienced spiritually has important echoes within the larger narrative of the Bible and the Church.

The Method

Jerome W. Berryman, *Teaching Godly Play: How to Mentor the Spiritual Development of Children*, 2009.

This book is the expanded and re-written second edition of a 1995 publication. It is the most complete statement of the method and, like the first edition, it is organized around what actually happens in a Godly Play room and combines that with background information about why adult mentors need to make certain moves when guiding children's spirituality. It also includes ways of evaluating one's practice of spiritual guidance and how to keep growing as a mentor.

The Theory of Spiritual Guidance

Jerome W. Berryman, *The Spiritual Guidance of Children: Montessori, Godly Play, and the Future*, 2013.

Godly Play reframes religious education as spiritual guidance. *The Spiritual Guidance of Children* relates this mentoring to the core of our spiritual identity (Chapter 4, "Godly Play and the Center Point"). The development of this core across the lifespan is also traced (Chapter 5, "The Center Point and Spiritual Maturity"). The book concludes that the guidance of children in Godly Play is fundamentally a matter of spiritual blessing between children and adults.

The Spiritual Guidance of Children describes Godly Play as an open but grounded approach to religion. It is deeply rooted in Christianity, but it is open and respectfully appreciates other religions. If children are deeply rooted in a particular religion, then they can understand other religions and discuss differences from depth to depth. When children are grounded but open, they can walk in another person's shoes because they have shoes of their own.

The View of Children's Spirituality

David Hay with Rebecca Nye, *The Spirit of the Child* (Revised ed.), 2006.

The Spirit of the Child was first published in 1998. The revised edition was published eight years later. David Hay began as a zoologist and worked on marine expeditions with Alister Hardy while as student at Aberdeen. Hay died in 2014 at the age of seventy-nine. Among many honors and publications, he was an early director of the Religious Experience Research Unit at Oxford, which helped establish religious experience as a viable subject for empirical research. This now classic book has three parts. It begins with an orientation to what spirituality is and why it is important. The second part describes a study of children's language about spirituality, conducted by Rebecca Nye, which established that children's spirituality is a kind of *relational consciousness* such as with the deep self, others, God, and the world.

The third part of the book is a reflection by Hay about what was discovered in Nye's early study, and how the nurturing of the child's spirit might take place in the English school system. Hay asserts that the suppression of children's spirituality in many school settings needs to be remedied, because spirituality continues to be important to children and it contributes to their health.

Rebecca Nye, *Children's Spirituality: What It Is and Why It Matters,* 2009.

Rebecca Nye's *Children's Spirituality* is well grounded in the countless questions people ask about children's spirituality. Dr. Nye, a child psychologist and a Godly Play trainer in the United Kingdom, discusses children's spirituality in a way that is detailed, concise, and easily understood.

The second half of the book is focused on the ways in which adults can nurture a child's spiritual life. Nye uses the SPIRIT acronym (Space, Process, Imagination, Relationship, Intimacy, Trust) to discuss six things adults should be aware of when engaged in the spiritual guidance of children.

A Sense of Maturity

Jerome W. Berryman, *Becoming Like a Child: The Curiosity of Maturity beyond the Norm*, 2017.

Maturity beyond the norm is about a kind of maturity that is different from the accumulation of years. It is a maturity found in children as well as adults. Life is conceived of as the flowing river of the creative process. Our creativity flows between the limits of rigidity and chaos, which shape and are shaped by our lives. The riverbanks need to be in touch with each other as openness and form for creativity to flow, but if one gets stuck in either rigidity or chaos the flow is frustrated. This kind of maturity is the long-term goal of Godly Play, and it was conceived of by using Godly Play as a research method to understand it.

Godly Play in the Home

Jerome W. Berryman, *Stories of God: Godly Play in the Home*, 2018.

This book will show how to use the knowledge gained from over forty years of work with children in Godly Play and apply it to what can be done at home from infancy to late childhood and beyond. It combines the perspective of history about parenting and Christian practice with many specific things to do to make one's spiritual practice with children at home a deeply playful and rooted experience of religion in the family.

This book is designed to stand on its own or to connect home practices with what is done in a more formal way involving the rich experience of a Godly Play room located in a church, school, or other setting.

Concluding Remarks about the Foundational Literature

This is only a summary of the foundational literature for Godly Play. This field is expanding as the discussion between science and religion continues and as Godly Play expands throughout the world.

Appendix B: The Spiral Curriculum for Godly Play

The following outline of the curriculum is organized in two ways. First, the Core Lessons, the Extensions, Enrichments, and Synthesis Lessons are laid out horizontally in parallel columns. The parallel columns are also grouped vertically according to the four key genres, as well as the lessons after the Biblical era, and lessons for the home and other settings. Each lesson has a number beside it to indicate which volume of *The Complete Guide to Godly Play* you can locate the lesson (unless the lesson is "in development"). A discussion of definitions with a brief discussion about each kind of lesson concludes this overview.

There are still materials and presentations being developed in the Godly Play room at the Center for the Theology of Childhood in Denver, but this overview provides a schematic look at the totality of the curriculum, as it now stands, so future details and improvements can be added in a coherent way to this overview.

Sacred Stories

A Sacred Story is one in which God has the primary role. We tell the stories of how people met God in Creation, with the patriarchs, in the Exodus, at Sinai, in the Temple, in the Prophets' visions, by encountering Jesus, and in other ways.

The Holy Family—This presentation sits on the Focal Shelf Unit in the center on the top shelf. It includes dimensions of all four genres, since it is a story, a liturgical experience, is parabolic, and invites contemplative silence. This presents the axis of the Christian language system by its concise integration of the birth, death, and resurrection of our Lord in a way open to the future. An Extension Lesson for the Holy Family is Mary, the Mother of Jesus.

CORE PRESENTATIONS	EXTENSIONS	ENRICHMENTS	SYNTHESIS
(3–6, 6–9, 9–12 years)	(6–9, 9–12 years)	(6–9, 9–12 years)	(9–12 years)
The Holy Family (2)			
The Holy Bible (2)		Books of the Bible (2)	
Creation (2)	Falling Apart (6)		
The Ark & the Flood (2)			
The Great Family (2)	Abraham (6) Sarah (6) Jacob (6) Joseph (6)		*Sacred Story Synthesis* (4)
Exodus (2)	Moses (6) Joseph (6)		
The Ten Best Ways (2)	Moses (6)		
The Ark and the Tent (2)	Ruth (6) Samuel (6) David (6)		

Sacred Stories *(continued)*

CORE PRESENTATIONS	EXTENSIONS	ENRICHMENTS	SYNTHESIS
(3–6, 6–9, 9–12 years)	(6–9, 9–12 years)	(6–9, 9–12 years)	(9–12 years)
The Ark and the Temple (2)	David (6)		
The Exile & Return (2)	Isaiah (6) Jeremiah (6) Ezekiel (6) Jonah (6)		
The Prophets (2)	Elijah (6) Isaiah (6) Jeremiah (6) Ezekiel (6) Jonah (2)		
Wisdom (in development)	Job (6) Daniel (6)		*Sacred Story Synthesis (4)*
Psalms (in development)	David (6)		
The Greatest Parable (8)	Miracles (in development) Mary (8)		
Jesus and the Twelve (4)	Peter (in development)		
Jesus and the Women (in development)			
Saul Changes (4)	Paul's Travels & Letters (4)		

Liturgical Action

Liturgy means literally, "the work of the people." Liturgy helps express inner and outer existential realities in a way that others can participate in the Godly Play approach. This includes lessons about Baptism and Holy Eucharist, as well as lessons about the liturgical seasons (Advent, Lent, Easter, and Pentecost).

CORE PRESENTATIONS (3–6, 6–9, 9–12 years)	EXTENSIONS (6–9, 9–12 years)	ENRICHMENTS (6–9, 9–12 years)	SYNTHESIS (9–12 years)
The Circle of the Church Year (mounted on wall) (2)			
The Circle of the Church Year (2)			
Advent I–IV & Christmas (3) Epiphany (3)	Mary (8)	Mystery of Christmas (3)	
Holy Baptism (3)			
Faces of Easter (4)		Mystery of Easter (4) Jesus & Jerusalem (8) Legend of Easter Egg (4) (developed after Biblical time)	*Liturgical Synthesis* (8)
Knowing Jesus in a New Way (8)	Mystery of Pentecost (4)		
The Good Shepherd World Communion (4)			
The Synagogue and the Upper Room (4)	Symbols of the Holy Eucharist (4)		
Circle of the Holy Eucharist (4)			

Parables

A parable is a kind of metaphor that uses short narrative fiction to reference a transcendent symbol, which in the Gospels is generally the Kingdom of heaven or Jesus. The Godly Play approach to parables includes six guiding parables in gold boxes, parables about parables, side-by-sides, and the Parable Synthesis Lessons (which include all the Parables of Jesus, his "I am" statements, and the Parable Games). The materials are generally flat to keep them more "open" than the three-dimensional materials used for the Sacred Stories.

CORE PRESENTATIONS	EXTENSIONS	ENRICHMENTS	SYNTHESIS
(3–6, 6–9, 9–12 years)	(6–9, 9–12 years)	(6–9, 9–12 years)	(9–12 years)
Parable of the Good Shepherd (3)		Side-by-Sides (3)	
Parable of the Great Pearl (3)		Parable of Parables (3)	
Parable of the Sower (3)		The Deep Well (3)	*Parable Synthesis* (3)
Parable of the Leaven (3)			
Parable of the Mustard Seed (3)			
Parable of the Good Samaritan (3)			

Contemplative Silence

This genre of classical Christian language is found in the way the lessons are presented. The mindfulness, measured pace, and leaving pauses contribute to this. The Prayers and reflection during the feast are also examples.

CORE PRESENTATIONS	EXTENSIONS	ENRICHMENTS	SYNTHESIS
(3–6, 6–9, 9–12 years)	(6–9, 9–12 years)	(6–9, 9–12 years)	(9–12 years)
The children are the "silence materials." The materials in the room must be silent. The children are the only ones in the room who can choose to be silent. Finally, there is a step in the presentation of "The Greatest Parable" (Volume 8, pp. 24–62) that is explicitly silent.			Contemplative Silence Synthesis (3)

After the Biblical Era

These are sometimes called the "afterwards" lessons. They are about things and events that took place after the Biblical era.

CORE PRESENTATIONS (3–6, 6–9, 9–12 years)	EXTENSIONS (6–9, 9–12 years)	ENRICHMENTS (6–9, 9–12 years)	SYNTHESIS (9–12 years)
The Part That Hasn't Been Written Yet (4)			
The Crosses (4)			
The Church (8)			
Intro. to the Communion of Saints OR Extended Intro. for children 6–12 (7)	Thomas Aquinas (7) Valentine (7) Patrick (7) Catherine of Siena (7) Julian of Norwich (7) Columba (7) Elizabeth of Portugal (7) Augustine of Hippo (7) Teresa of Calcutta (7) Teresa of Avila (7) Margaret of Scotland (7) Nicholas, Bishop of Myra (7) The Story of the Child's Own Saint (7) The Story of the Child's Own Life (7)		*Afterward Synthesis**

*The Afterwards Synthesis is for older children, nine to twelve years. They are taken into the church and are invited to walk around in the church as a group with the co-teachers.

At each significant part of the interior architecture the group stops and the storyteller invites wondering about where each part comes from. The stories in the windows are discussed. The altar/table placement is discussed. The crossing is discussed. What is behind and above the altar/table is discussed. The use of symbols is discussed. Each point of interest is touched, and talked about. The group then goes outside the church to look at the exterior architectural shape of the church and what it says to them and to the community around it.

Special Presentation for the Godly Play Room

The Right Rite: Choosing the Appropriate Liturgical Action for Life's Experiences (in development).

Special Presentations for the Home and Other Settings

These materials and presentations are designed especially for the home, mostly to be done around the table, like the Jewish Seder. They are also useful in additional settings, such as presenting the creation story on camping trips and other family outings.

These lessons resemble lessons found in a Godly Play room, but they are smaller and the presentations are much shorter. This is so the lesson can be laid out on a table when the "family" (however one may define that . . .) is gathered for a meal. The lessons draw the family story into the Biblical Story. Adults or older children lead these small liturgies, which are accessible to all ages with a minimum amount of preparation by the leaders. Instructions about how to use these lessons at home can be found in Jerome Berryman's book, *Stories of God: Godly Play in the Home* (2018).

Advent/Christmas: The Story of God with Us

Lent/Easter: The Story of God's Redemptive Love

Eastertide/Pentecost: The Story of God Creating Within

Creation: The Story of God's Creating

The Parable of the Good Shepherd: The Story of God's Nature

The Circle of the Church Year: The Story of God's Wholeness

Defining the Kinds of Lessons

"Core Lessons" are the key Sacred Story, Liturgical Action, Parable, and Contemplative Silence lessons. An example from the Sacred Story genre is "Creation."

The Sacred Stories follow the key events noted by Samuel Terrien's, *The Elusive Presence*, which provides the Biblical theology for Godly Play. The Liturgical Action presentations follow the liturgical year. The Parables follow the loosely organized collections in the Synoptic Gospels. The Contemplative Silence genre may be found in the way the lessons are presented, the organization of the room. The children are the main embodiment of this genre.

"**Extensions**" extend the Core Lessons. They expand not only Sacred Stories but also the Liturgical and Parable lessons. An example is the story of "Ruth," which helps extend the narratives of "The Temple" and "The Ark and the Tent" by implicitly connecting them. The "Ruth" lesson joins "Samuel" and "David" to do this. All three types of extensions sit on the shelves below these lessons, which are displayed on the top shelf in the Godly Play room.

The materials for this type of lesson are all placed on strips (with the exception of Ruth and Jonah), as they are told, because they can be laid alongside the Core Lesson, literally extending out from them along the line of the story. The strips can all be joined together to connect the Core Lesson for a long timeline of the Biblical narrative. This is an impressive lesson, because the long line will probably not fit in the Godly Play room. It will have to be put together in the hallway or a larger room by a group of interested children.

"**Enrichment**" Lessons do not extend but enrich or deepen the Core Lessons. This kind of lesson goes over the same material that is in the Core Lesson from a different angle or in more detailed way. An example is using the model of Jerusalem to re-tell what was said about Holy Week during the presentation of "The Faces." This adds detail explicitly and implicitly by setting the story more securely in the city and its geographical setting of valleys and hills.

"**Afterwards**" lessons involve events and symbols that are not part of the Biblical era. An example is the variety of crosses that have been developed since the original Roman cross Jesus died on. Another example is the lesson about "The Church."

"**Synthesis**" Lessons make a synthesis of key lessons in the four genres. The Synthesis Lesson for the Sacred Stories integrates key narratives to make a lesson about the Holy Trinity. The Synthesis Lessons (there are two) for the Parables synthesize all of the parables from the Synoptic Gospels and the "I–Am" statements from the Gospel of John around a series of questions about the collection of parables and what they create as a whole. The Synthesis Lesson for the Liturgical Action Lessons draws together the liturgical lessons into a series of circles. The Synthesis Lesson for the Contemplative Silence genre takes the older children into the Church to sit in silence and to see if they become more aware of God's presence. Then they return to the Godly Play room to wonder about what happened.

The Synthesis Lesson of the Afterwards lessons doesn't represent a particular genre of Biblical communication. It builds on the four key genres of the foundational Christian communication system and they evoke how this foundation has worked itself out in the history of the church. The Synthesis Lesson for this kind of communication, then, is to take the older children on tours of the Church's interior and exterior to see how what is inside and outside draws on and evokes both the primary, Biblical communication, and what has developed since then. An example is the shape of the Church itself, what it communicates in its particular features, and what it communicates generally as a whole.

Discussion

There are, of course, overlaps in the aforementioned definitions. "Knowing Jesus in a New Way" is a good example. It is a Sacred Story, but it is also a Core Liturgical Action Lesson, because it follows the liturgical structure of Eastertide and parallels the way the lessons for "The Faces" prepare for Easter during Lent. This is not merely a story about Jesus in the first century, but it is organized to follow the liturgical year to bring the experience into the present, rather than being relegated to history. The artwork is different from "The Faces," because Jesus' presence is suggested by the faces of the disciples rather than his own. The disciples are slowly beginning to understand what the empty tomb means for them as we do today. They are in the same position relative to Jesus, as we are, as we move from being sheep to shepherds.

"The Mystery of Pentecost" is an extension of "Knowing Jesus in a New Way," because it extends this narrative by adding the Tower of Babel to the narrative of Pentecost. The loss of a common language and experience of God is told in the story of the Tower of Babel, while in "The Mystery of Pentecost" a renewed sense of unity is expressed that Jesus' presence gives those who communicate as Christians. This theme is also part of the background for "The Greatest Parable."

"The Greatest Parable" is a Sacred Story about the public ministry of Jesus, but it might also be thought of as an extension of "The Faces." It extends this Core Lesson, but it is more importantly the culmination of the Sacred Story about God's elusive presence that began with "Creation," so it is listed as a Core Lesson. "The Greatest Parable" not only tells the story of Jesus' public ministry but also acknowledges that the whole Christian language system flows out of Jesus' life, death, and resurrection, as well as his coming again. This lesson, then, has the whole Godly Play room as its extension and enrichment. This is why it is the most curious box in the whole room.

Another overlap can be illustrated by "Jesus and Jerusalem," thought of as an Enrichment Lesson. A schematic model of Jerusalem is used to trace

Jesus' movements during Holy Week. It could be considered an extension of "The Faces," because it adds a few details to Jesus' journey during Holy Week. The model and map, however, do not add *substantially* to "The Faces." Instead, it provides a sensorial telling of what happened, using much the same language as used in "The Faces," so it is more an Enrichment than an Extension Lesson.